MW00700770

THE DULUTH GRILL COOK BOOK

Volume II

THE DULUTH GRILL COOKBOOK II

WRITTEN BY **ROBERT LILLEGARD**
PHOTOGRAPHY BY **ROLF HAGBERG**

Duluth Grill Publishing
118 South 27th Avenue West
Duluth, MN 55806
218-726-1150
info@DuluthGrill.com

THE DULUTH GRILL COOKBOOK II

Printed in the United States of America
10 9 8 7 6 5 4 3 2 1 0 First Edition

ISBN-13: 978-0-9886112-1-4

All photos by Rolf Hagberg except where otherwise noted.
Designed by Kollath Graphic Design

TABLE of CONTENTS

LIST *of* RECIPES

CONDIMENTS & SAUCES

BEVERAGES

BREAKFAST

SOUPS AND STARTERS

Vegetarian: 🍁 Vegan: **V** Gluten-Free: ★ Fast & Easy: **FE**

SIDES

BIG HEARTY ENTREES

DESSERTS

PRAISE FOR THE DULUTH GRILL

"That is comfort food 101. You sure have a knack for pulling it off and for making it tasty."

— ***Guy Fieri, Diners, Drive-Ins and Dives***

"The Hanson family's commitment to sustainable practices is evident all across the menu—goodbye to can openers, hello to family farms—and it extends to the parking lot, where herbs and vegetables are cultivated in raised garden beds. The lengthy menu does good things with basics like eggs and bacon, buttermilk pancakes and BLTs before moving on to far more inspired fare. If only breakfast-all-day was this good everywhere."

— ***Rick Nelson, Minneapolis Star Tribune***

"It's one thing to go all locavore when you're in California; it's another thing entirely when you're on the shore of Lake Superior, which freezes solid in the winter. In its own way, though, Duluth Grill may even be more important, demonstrating that this kind of idealism isn't just for urban sophisticates willing to pay $25 for appetizers."

— ***Russ Parsons, Los Angeles Times***

"What's not to like about Duluth Grill? It's a truck-stop style diner in the friendly West End neighborhood that buys from local farmers and grows some of its vegetables around its parking lot in raised-bed gardens. Duluth Grill is much more than a simple breakfast joint, but readers of *Perfect Duluth Day* strongly agreed in a recent poll that it is indeed the best breakfast restaurant in the area."

— ***Paul Lundgren, Perfect Duluth Day***

"The odds seemed to be against this place when it first opened. Duluth Grill is an old Embers restaurant in a rather bleak, industrial section off interstate 35. But a few years ago, the owner tried something different—a new emphasis on locally grown foods with that fresh from the ground flavor. It's become a reason for people to venture into a part of the city that they wouldn't have visited otherwise."

— ***Mike Binkley, WCCO***

"I think the word 'foodie' is the most overused and misused word in the English language. A foodie isn't someone who loves food and adds truffle oil to stuff. A foodie is someone who truly understands food, what it can do and how it can make you feel. Robert and his friends at The Duluth Grill certainly qualify—but better than foodies they are really passionate people working together to create really delicious food AND are clearly having a blast doing it! Just like Volume I, this book is fun to thumb through, fun to read, and rewarding to cook from. The love of food, friends, and family is palpable in every single page, and what could be more delicious than that?"

—***Ana Quincoces***, *cookbook author, TV personality, and creator of* ***Skinny Latina***

"The Hanson family's philosophy of seasonal cooking is one we all need to embrace, not only for the love of taking care of the planet, but also for the enjoyment of root to stem cooking at its best. It's rare to find such dedication in sourcing stock and trade, as the Hansons do. The efforts show through in their foods and flavors. The great thing about a restaurant cookbook is that the chefs have made the recipes thousands of time so they know they work. I enjoy the Duluth Grill both for its commitment to the locavore philosophy before it was popular, and that its food tastes like home cooking—because it is"

—***Arlene Coco***, *food writer and owner of* ***Prairie Kitchen Specialty Foods***

"Never mind that the Duluth Grill is a standout independent restaurant of the North whose cookbook would be a perfect addition to your shelf, what turns it into a must have page-turner is the honest and engaging, and often cheeky, voice of its writer Robert Lillegard. A true eater and foodist with a penchant for chicken jokes and headers like Where Did All The Fish Go?, his words help this surpass a simple collection of recipes with farmer profiles, giving us a real and sometimes hilarious slice of the restaurant world and Northern eating life. You will read this one cover to cover."

—***Stephanie March***, *Dining Editor for Mpls. St. Paul Magazine*

"It's of great pleasure and excitement to have the privilege of endorsing the most recent cookbook on The Duluth Grill. It's extremely on trend as well as socially and culturally beneficial to the American public. Even R.D. Thomas, founder of Wendy's and a person I look at as one of my mentors, told me in 1981 that by no latter than 1995 the menu trend in the restaurant industry will become much more bent towards nutrition and portion sizes. He was right on target with his prediction! Congratulations with the outstanding work in putting together your newest cookbook."

—***Doug Sheley***, *Founder & CEO of D'Lites of America*

"The Duluth Grill bravely cooks up wonderful adventures that extend beyond the kitchen. The typical recipe of what a restaurant should be is thrown out the window and takes flight with permaculture panache. Don't just go for the amazing food and vibe but give yourself a tour of their exotic edible landscaping. A Duluth destination with great gastronomics! They continue to blaze new paths with wild abandon. Locavores and organic lovers satiated in their wake now have a tome to take home."

—***Chad Johnson***, *Permaculturalist, Spirit Mountain Farm, Holzer AgroEcology*

DEDICATION

This book is dedicated to one of our mentors: Donald James.
Through his fearless, quirky, creative and occasionally child-like
approach he opened our eyes and our minds to quality.
This is the reason to do what we do.

—Jaima and Tom

AUTHOR'S DEDICATION

This book is dedicated to Alicia, my favorite wife, who went to a bunch
of book signings with me when she was pregnant.

—Robert Lillegard

FOREWORD
by BEA OJAKANGAS

It was several years ago that I visited the back yard of the Hanson home on the West hillside of Duluth with a group of *Les Dames d'Escoffier*. Truthfully, the project they had embarked on looked a bit impossible. There was a huge outdoor fish tank in the back yard. In Duluth? When the winter temps can get in the minus 20s and 30s? "They must be kidding," I thought. How do you heat almost 5,000 gallons of water? Then, they have all these veggies growing around in the summertime. How do they do that? They have managed to pull it all off with lots of ingenuity and perseverance. Today it is a virtual hobby farm!

Bea Ojakangas

Then, there's the location—just off I-35 on 27th West in a location that appears to be like a glorified gas station stop. The dozen of us, or so, were in awe. You'd expect the typical burgers and fries. The menu offers a lot more—try the walnut tacos! The food is organic, vegetarian or vegan if that's what you like, but there are plenty of choices for the carnivore. Local favorites show up on the menu, too, like beef pasties so popular on the Iron Range.

I ordered a beet lemonade made with beet juice and homemade lemonade, spiked with a few celery-like lovage and mint leaves and there are other refreshing choices. Even though there are no beer or wine or other alcoholic beverage choices, the place is packed day in and day out. We've found that the best time to go for dinner is in the late afternoon to enjoy comfort foods like and homemade desserts like banana cream pie and cheesecake.

The Duluth Grill has been on the Food Network's *Diners, Drive-Ins, and Dives* with Guy Fieri. Whether you're a vegan, vegetarian, or gluten-free there are meal plans for you. So if you would like to replicate some of the Duluth Grill menu items—they are well presented in this cookbook with beautiful photos. DG

***Bea Ojakangas** is a member of the **James Beard Cookbook Hall of Fame**. She has baked with Julia Child and Martha Stewart, won the **Pillsbury Bakeoff**, and written 29 cookbooks.*

A WORD FROM THE AUTHOR

As a writer, I get nervous when starting big new projects. Last cookbook, I had researched and researched and I just couldn't get going. So I started making jokes about chickens. The rest of the book kind of flowed from there. This book came together pretty much the same way and I hope you enjoy it.

—***Robert Lillegard***

A WORD *from* TOM & JAIMA

2016 marks the beginning of the 38th year that both Jaima and I have been in the restaurant business. The edition of this book really notes a time when the world keeps growing and changing.

I want to talk about Louis, Jeff, Dan, and the future of food in this market. As much as I can have a great, energized day, time will carry on and there will be a new generation.

I think the idea of doing a second cookbook really marks time in this business. It's the idea that we've got the next generation that is really running this restaurant today. We weren't that much older than Louis when we started the Duluth Grill. We had young kids like he does, we were in our thirties like he is. There's a time when you have to look at the longevity of your business. You realize that the question is whether you're going to carry on a tradition of service or let your business deteriorate.

I guess we have to go back to the why we're writing this cookbook. For me personally it's not about the success of selling it, though it's a huge investment. First of all, it's about journaling the history of the Duluth Grill.

If I look at our business over the 15 years it's almost like a child. In the beginning you had to wipe its mouth and change its diapers. As it gets a little older you let others handle some of that day-to-day work, but you still micromanage every decision. Now the restaurant is in its adolescence. By distancing ourselves, we're allowing it to mature and grow.

It's the same with our food. In the beginning we were

Don Doane, Whitney LeFebvre holding Willow LeFebvre, Dan LeFebvre, Caden (top) and Corbin (bottom) Petcoff, Jeff Petcoff, Darlyne Jansen (bottom), Julie Petcoff, Tony Jansen, Carolyn Hanson, Paul Hanson, Jaima Hanson, Tom Hanson, Peyton Hanson, Louis Hanson (top), Parker Hanson (bottom), Ashley Hanson

definitely working with standard fare, but trying to do it with a way that had care and concern. As we grew, we stuck our necks out a little with things like edamame and vegan main dishes. Now, people are looking for new and creative ideas. All the people that are "foodies," they're definitely wanting to know more about quality and more about preparation. I would say that the recipes in this book reflect that evolution.

I don't think we're trying to be something, this is just who we are. The longer we've done this, the more we're defining and understanding what our customer is looking for. We constantly re-evaluate what's selling and what's being rejected. We're trying to do our homework in researching what's trending and trying to bring it to Duluth.

In 2012 we put our first book out. Here it is three years later. You could look back on what's happened in the last three years, but you could never forecast it. That's one reason we're writing this book—to tell that story.

I also see this book as an opportunity. It all started with people asking for recipes, which we've always given out. But at this point in our history, a cookbook is not so much about self-promotion as it is about giving people what they want. If you go to a tourist attraction and there are no souvenirs, you say, "that was a historic experience, but I'm leaving with nothing". The customer wants to bring a piece of the restaurant home with them.

Finally, the book is about recognition. To orchestrate a team like we have it's critical for us to recognize our people. In the first book Jaima and I got a lot of credit. We were younger, people were busy doing their own thing, so the book was largely about us. Three years ago, I said 'we can't get any busier than we already are'. Here we're close to 75% busier than we were. To make it happen it takes a team of professionals. This book concentrates on our managers Dan, Louis, and Jeff and catering manager Don Doane, along with our suppliers and vendors (including our farm manager François). I think this book is our way of saying there's more than just the two of us running this thing. We're excited to be putting out a second cookbook filled with all new recipes. We're excited to be opening another restaurant and expanding catering. Most of all, we're excited to see a new generation take our place as leaders. We're trying to recognize that whatever you do is a short while, even if it's 50 years.

—***Jaima and Tom***

THREE-DAY MEAL PLANS

These recipes were chosen with vegans, vegetarians, and gluten-sensitive people in mind. Here are a few ideas for complete meals that fit your lifestyle. While the Duluth Grill philosophy leans towards scratch-made food, there's also a meal plan if you're looking for something fast and easy!

VEGAN

Day One

BREAKFAST

Besan Chilla 48
Pineapple Salsa 16
Cashew Sour Cream 15

LUNCH

Peanut Soup 56
Bread

DINNER

Walnut Tacos 86
Cuban Black Beans 91
Avocado Mango Sorbet 136

Day Two

BREAKFAST

Oatmeal
Blueberry jam 15

LUNCH

Hummus with Preserved Lemon 82
Marinated Kale 89

DINNER

Zucchini Minestrone 66
Quinoa Pilaf 85

Day Three

BREAKFAST

Cold Press Coffee With Vanilla Syrup and Coconut Milk 32

LUNCH

Kale and White Bean Soup 66

DINNER

Marinara Sauce 92
Pasta
Salad
Cilantro Lime Vinaigrette 19
Sugar Cookies 123

VEGETARIAN

Day One

BREAKFAST

Scones 42

LUNCH

Pumpkin Soup 58

DINNER

Ba-Beetza 98
Green Bean Casserole 84
Florentines 122

TESTED BY HOME COOKS

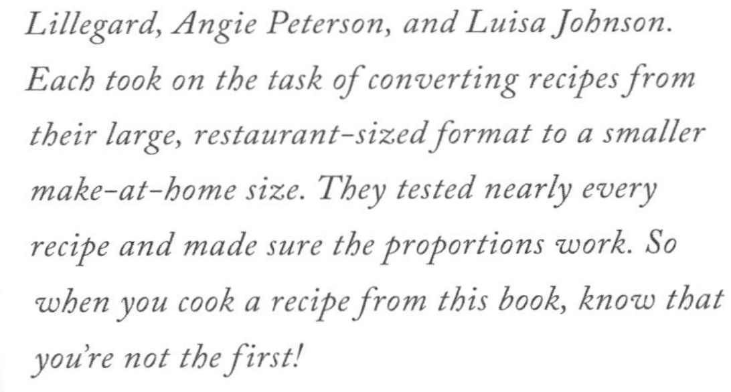

We wanted this cookbook to be easy and usable by the home cook. So, we got help from four local home cooks—Sarah Chambers, Michael Lillegard, Angie Peterson, and Luisa Johnson. Each took on the task of converting recipes from their large, restaurant-sized format to a smaller make-at-home size. They tested nearly every recipe and made sure the proportions work. So when you cook a recipe from this book, know that you're not the first!

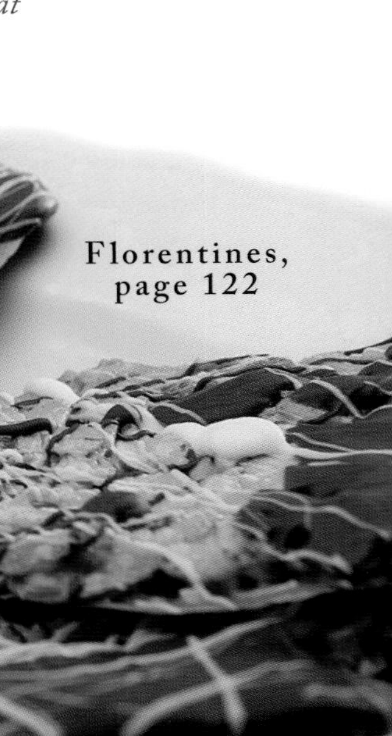

Florentines, page 122

MY JOURNEY THROUGH THE DULUTH GRILL MENU

When my husband and I said we would be testers for the second Duluth Grill cookbook, I don't think we knew what we were getting into. We both love to cook, but lead busy and unpredictable lives.

At the beginning, I was off work recovering from a broken collarbone and thought I would have more time to do the recipes. My injury did hamper my ability to lift and carry things so we got off to a slow start. Then, to compound things, we started a remodel project that had been on hold over the summer.

You find a lot of interesting things when you remodel a 97 year old house. However, you do not find things like "how many cups are in a pound of blueberries?" and "how do you divide 3/4 of a cup into fourths?" Thank goodness for the Internet! It helped us answer a lot of questions, like "What is a *chiffonade*?", "How do I 'temper' eggs?", and of course "Why is my cake flat?"

When we did find time to work on the recipes, our labors were occasionally fraught with peril. We sliced a few fingers, got a few burns, and almost destroyed one of our prized antique cast iron skillets when trying to blacken peppers. The first time we made the Black Beans with Mango Salsa, an ingredient that was supposed to be added at the end didn't make it into the beans. Seeing as it was a main ingredient, the beans tasted a little flat. When we discovered the omission and made the beans again, this time *with* the ingredient, they were a lot better.

We sliced a few fingers, got a few burns, and almost destroyed one of our prized antique cast iron skillets when trying to blacken peppers.

But the layered carrot cake caused us the most distress. After three failures and multiple trips to the Duluth Grill to see if we were on the right track, I finally got it right well after midnight. I fed the whole cake to our friends (we were getting discouraged) but as I was writing up the recipe, I kept smelling it anyway. I thought to myself "after making this cake 4 times, you're cracking up!" Then I realized that failures 1, 2 and 3 were still sitting in the pans on the table right next to me.

Thankfully we genuinely liked just about everything we were assigned. There were some definite gems in there, such as my beloved Pickled Jalapenos and the extremely tasty Bison Stuffed Peppers. The creamy textures of the Broccoli Cheese Soup and the Cheesy Ham and Potato Soup are divine. I even believe that, in a few years, when the anguish of the debacle wears off, I will enjoy the Carrot Layer Cake. DG

Grateful for the experience,
— ***Sarah Chambers***

THE REAL HOUSEWIVES OF MIAMI, GOVERNOR DAYTON'S MANSION, AND ONE DANGEROUS DRIVE

A BEHIND-THE-SCENES LOOK AT THE FIRST BOOK

If Tom Hanson, owner of the Duluth Grill, gets an idea, watch out. It's going to happen

Plant an urban farm in west Duluth? Check. Dig up the back parking lot for a community funded orchard/rain garden? Check. So when he started talking to me about doing a cookbook, it was all just a matter of time.

The governor's mansion, the Real Housewives of Miami, the Heinz lawsuit scare, all that would come later. In the beginning, it was just me, the book, and a quickly-expanding budget

One of Tom's favorite stories about the book is when we hired photographer Rolf Hagberg. I know it's his favorite because he makes fun of me about it all the time. Here's what I apparently said:

"We used to use this guy for the magazine, but we stopped because he was too expensive. But he's the best. We have to go with him."

To which Tom thought: HOW much is this going to cost me?

To his credit, he did end up going with the suggestion. We're glad we picked Rolf, who for the record IS the best. For a designer we went with Rick Kollath, because he worked out with me at my kettlebell gym (strong guy!), and also because he had a lot of book experience

That experience ended up making a big difference in October 2012, when it came time to start getting the book printed. We had spent the last thirteen months puttering around, getting photos and text, and generally being late and foot-draggy about putting the recipes together. Now Christmas was coming, and we wanted the book ASAP. But the printing company had other ideas.

"We used to use this guy for the magazine, but we stopped because he was too expensive. But he's the best. We have to go with him."

"One of the big memories was when we were talking to the [designer]," Jeff Petcoff says. "He said 'rushing it would have been two months ago. This *is* turbo-speed'. You don't know those things unless you do it every day."

It was an anxious time, though. We had a big pile of pre-orders and I was getting calls from Jeff or Tom every few days just politely inquiring when

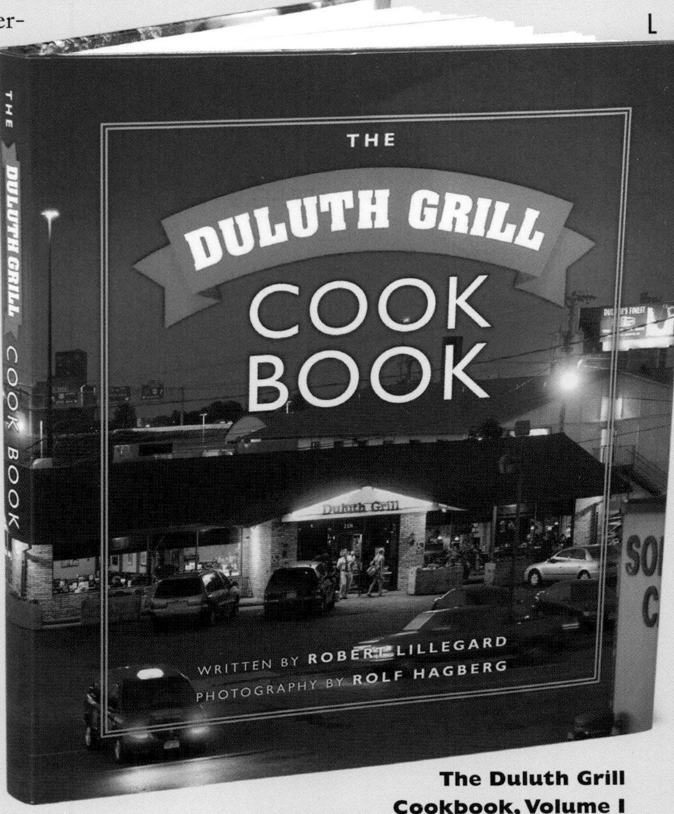

The Duluth Grill Cookbook, Volume I
(though we didn't know it at the time).

exactly the book might be coming back from the printers.

Sometime after Thanksgiving, things came to a head. They wanted to know that the deadline I promised was firm.

I paused. This was one of those take-a-deep-breath moments.

"If it doesn't come through," I said, "I will loan you half the printing cost. Until June."

I had personally guaranteed an interest-free, six-month $9,000 loan out of my own pocket. Printing guy, I thought, you'd better come through.

Meanwhile, our hapless printing guy Tobbi was dealing with struggles of his own. The snows were falling, the wind was blowing, and the roads were iced slick. And in early December, Tobbi inched his little car down to Minneapolis to get us a couple of boxes of books.

Success!

Tobbi's return trip took something like four hours. For the first and hopefully last time, I spent an evening standing in a kitchen putting books into boxes for our pre-orders. The rest of the books arrived a few days later by truck. It was a smash hit.

But our adventure was far from over.

Later that winter, I woke up around eight, and saw a text on my phone from Tom—sent at 4:20 that morning.

"I found something in the book so I pulled them from the shelves. call me"

I may or may not have panicked. Could there be a worse message for a writer to get? But when I called I went from worried to confused. Tom was concerned that we could get a lawsuit from Heinz, since we had commented in our book that the ketchup had changed so much from the original Heinz would probably turn over in his grave.

"Oh, Tom," I said. "That's not going to happen."

We put the books back on the shelf.

Fast forward two weeks. Voicemail from Jaima.

"Heinz called," she said. "Their rep is coming. I'm here by myself."

Ummmm. Ok, so there *was* a worse message a writer could get.

It was a long afternoon, though it probably felt even longer for Jaima than it did for me. But to cut straight to the chase: nothing happened. The Heinz rep was on a social call, and didn't mention the book once.

What more is there to tell? My friend Ana Quincoces ended up becoming one of the Real Housewives of Miami and pushing our book to her tens of thousands of followers. Another friend spotted our little book on the coffee table of Governor Dayton's mansion. We met with Beatrice Ojakangas, Duluth's most famous food writer, who said she thought it looked great.

And the fun only continued. We were approached by Barnes and Noble and placed in all their stores in Minnesota and in Wisconsin, then did a multi-city book tour including an appearance on Madison, Wisconsin's TV news. We got some advice from 3-times New York Times bestselling author and former American Apparel marketing director Ryan Holliday. We saw our book sold in Norway, got on a blog in Canada, and handed a copy to Slovenia's foremost all-female polka group (hey—baby steps). It's been crazy and it's been beautiful and it's been a headache and we're selling thousands and thousands. There's only one thing that worries me…

We've got to do it all again. DG

An earlier version of this article was published in Lake Superior Magazine. See, even our press coverage is local!

Ana Quincoces is the creator of the Skinny Latina food line, a 3x cookbook author, a former Real Housewife of Miami, and a fan of the author's baby on Twitter

MATT AND SARA WEIK: YKER ACRES

Matt and Sara Weik are pretty much your typical suburban couple—the 9-to-5 job, the 2.5 kids, the 30-year mortgage. Just replace the 30-year mortgage with a house Matt built himself, the 2.5 kids with one really, really good bike racer who's touring in Europe, and the 9-to-5 with "self-employed pig farmers", and you've got it. But for Sara, who used to assist at home births as a doula, and Matt, who raced sled dogs professionally, life has never been about fitting in.

"We don't do a lot of social things so I'm not reminded of it," Sara says. "When we do go in the 'outside world' then I do realize. [But] this is our normal. It's very freeing to not have to worry if you're being normal enough!"

Matt is actually a third generation pig farmer. He used to spend his summers in Iowa with his pig farming uncles. But he didn't get into the business right away. He mushed professionally in races like the 938-mile Iditarod in Alaska and raised sled dogs as well. Later, he owned a trucking and a landscaping business. One day, Josey, their only son, needed some spending money. A lot of guys would have suggested a lemonade stand, but the Weiks had other ideas.

"The pig business was started by my son," Matt says. "He was 12, 13. He wanted to make more money so we bought him 12 feeder pigs and he sold them as pork shares."

This little side business turned out to be, as people say in northern Minnesota, "quite the deal". Those 12 pigs turned to 30 and when a restaurant owner in Minneapolis asked Matt to raise 10 pigs a month for him, the rest was history.

"The pig business was started by my son. He wanted to make more money so we bought him 12 feeder pigs and he sold them as pork shares."

"Ever since my wife and I were married, growing food's been our thing," Matt says. "The market created itself at the right time when we were ready to do it."

Matt and Josey Weik

While a muddy field isn't most people's definition of paradise (if it's yours, I have a field to sell you), pigs love it. YKer Acres pigs grow up with 1,000 square feet of space and plenty of good feed like legumes. Low stress lives lead to better quality meat and Matt and Sara are out mucking and watering them rain or shine. Pigs are social animals, and by the time they're ready for harvest, Matt says there's a little bit of regret.

"Every animal that comes off our farm, it's sad," Weik says. "We are respectful and remorseful. [But] we realize that's one more animal that lived a really good existence while they are here."

The farm has gotten to the stage where it can produce 5,000 pounds of quality pork per month and that number is only set to increase. Matt and Sara do most of the work themselves, from feeding the pigs to making sales calls. And when it's time for the new baby pigs to arrive Sara brings her extensive experience as a doula to the table.

"I will have to say, there are a lot of similarities," Sara says. "Pigs are very intelligent animals, and they labor a lot like a mom does."

Then she went into a lot of detail, which was pretty hilarious, but possibly not a great fit for a cookbook ("Sara! People are trying to eat here!"). Suffice it to say that she's carried over her compassion for new life from people to pigs. And even though, yes, the pigs do eventually get killed and eaten, it's important to treat them well in the meantime.

Matt and Sara Weik are creating something new—and having a lot of fun in the process

"Of all the animals to really concentrate on and [have] concern about treatment of is the pig, because they are so intelligent," Sara says. "This is a great place to start."

It takes a pretty exceptional team to take on the US pig farming industry and come out swinging. But by responding to customer demand for humanely treated, great tasting pork, Matt and Sara Weik are creating something new—and having a lot of fun in the process.

"I don't fit into a box very well," Matt says. "I'm always thinking of something new and a better way to do it." DG

HE DIDN'T START THE FIRE

CATERING AT THE DULUTH GRILL

One day a few years ago, catering manager Don Doane's childhood friend Steve came to visit him at the restaurant. The two went for a walk in Canal Park and it seemed like every other person they met was saying hi to Don—thanking him for successful catering jobs, giving him a high five or just saying they were glad to see him.

"You're popular here," Steve said, clearly impressed. "But come visit me in Los Angeles, and you'll just be another face in the crowd."

A month later, Don took Steve up on his offer. To his astonishment, he was just as popular in Los Angeles. Even the mayor rolled down his window to say hello.

"I can't believe it," Steve said. "But I know one man you surely don't know. If I take you to Italy to see the Pope, then we'll be on equal ground."

So Don agreed. After a meal of pizza and gelato, the two wandered down to the Piazza San Pietro. The crowds murmured as the Pope came out on his balcony. And then people gasped as the Pope waved to Don to come up. Don left Steve in the crowd and a few minutes later he came out onto the balcony, smiling and waving at the crowd.

Really, who among us hasn't set a van on fire once or twice? It's one of those youthful mistakes everyone makes. And the way Don explains it, it does sound pretty reasonable.

When Don got back to Steve he found him unconscious.

"Steve!" Don said. "Wake up. What's wrong?"

Steve slowly opened his eyes.

"I could handle you knowing the Pope," he said. "But when a tourist turned to me and asked 'who's that guy in the funny hat next to Don Doane?', I lost it!"

This story is probably apocryphal, but it definitely does justice to the myth of Don. The Duluth Grill's catering manager likes food, sailing, and dealing with people, and not necessarily in that order. Don has been working in mass food service since 1981, when he was the director of dining services at a women's college. He's been focusing on catering since 2002 and started with the Duluth Grill in 2011.

The happy catering Chef, Don Doane

VETERANS EXHIBIT!
GENERATIONS

"We're going to do half a million this year," Don says. "The first four months I was here we did $55,000. That's a little bit of growth."

From the North Shore Scenic Railroad dining train to pig roasts to private catering for celebrities stopping by at Monaco Air, Don's seen it all. Often, catering ends up being a can-to-table situation. But at the Duluth Grill, the goal is to get the same scratch-made food people find at the restaurant out to events. That means a lot of prep work in the kitchen ahead of time and some careful juggling to transport it all. People are really responding and the Grill's catering business has almost quadrupled since Don started.

Now the bright white catering van is a frequent sight at Duluth events. Fortunately, it hasn't been set on fire. At least not frequently.

"They all blame me for trying to set the van on fire one night," Don says. "I still declare that it wasn't me."

Really, who among us hasn't set a van on fire once or twice? It's one of those youthful mistakes everyone makes. And the way Don explains it, it does sound pretty reasonable. It all started with a buffet down at the Great Lakes Aquarium on a cold, miserable night.

"We had to break a line down real fast because they were using that area," Don says. "I thought Tom knew what I was doing—I was just carrying the trays back so we could empty them. Tom just put them in the damn box, not knowing that the Sterno was still ablaze."

Don brings up a good point. If there's one thing you learn in Driver's Ed, it's never to put burning Sterno boxes into a van.

"The next thing I hear is Louis jumping into the van to put the fire out because one of the chafing boxes caught on fire," Don says. "Yeah, I haven't lived that one down." DG

Condiments & Sauces

GARLIC SPREAD

Vegetarian, Vegan, Gluten-Free

For young cloves who aspire to be fashion models, a garlic spread is second only to a garlic centerfold for building that all-important magazine portfolio. But this spread is so good it might make you the celebrity at your next party.

INGREDIENTS:

1 cup garlic

1/4 cup plus 1–2 Tbsp olive oil

1/2 tsp salt

1/2 tsp black pepper

DIRECTIONS:

- Preheat oven to 300°F.
- In a bowl lightly toss garlic, salt and pepper with 1–2 Tbsp olive oil (enough to lightly coat).
- Place on a baking sheet and cover with aluminum foil and bake for 60 minutes or until tender, stirring once half-way through.
- Place roasted garlic in a processor and puree until smooth adding olive oil as needed to make mixture smooth and spreadable.
- Serve immediately or refrigerate until ready to serve.
- Yields about 1 cup

CASHEW SOUR CREAM

Vegetarian, Vegan, Gluten Free, Fast and Easy

This is where you pull out the powerful blender. If your blender is weak or not getting this as creamy as you'd like, soak the cashews longer (up to four hours).

1/2 cup raw cashews (soaked 1 hour)

2 tablespoons water

1 teaspoon apple cider vinegar

1/2 teaspoon lemon juice

pinch salt

- Blend all ingredients in a high speed blender (vitamix) until completely smooth.
- Yield: 1/2 cup

PINEAPPLE SALSA

Vegetarian, Vegan, Gluten-Free, Fast and Easy

Salsa is one of the most popular raw recipes for good reason. It's supposed to be juicy, crunchy, and a little bit sour. This is a particularly good pick for someone who's allergic to tomatoes.

INGREDIENTS:

1 cup diced pineapple

1/2 cup diced cucumber

1/4 cup diced jicama

1/4 cup chopped cilantro leaves

1/4 cup brined red onion

1 tablespoon lime juice

1/4 minced, deseeded jalapeño pepper

pinch salt

DIRECTIONS:

- Peel and dice fruits and vegetables into 1/4-inch pieces (deseed cucumber and pepper).
- Combine all ingredients in mixing bowl.
- Yield: 2 cups

CHUTNEY

Vegetarian, Gluten-Free

A study by the Indian Institute of Technology found that while Western food is based on complementary flavors, Indian food is based on contrasting flavors—like sweet mangos, sour vinegar, and spicy chili powder in the same chutney. This makes for a punchy sauce that will liven up meat dishes or vegetable curries.

INGREDIENTS:

1/2 lb mangoes

1/4 cup honey

2 ounces brown sugar

1/4 cup cider vinegar

1/2 cup Craisins

2 Tbsp chopped ginger

2 tsp fresh lemon juice

1/2 tsp chili powder

1/4 tsp nutmeg

1/4 tsp salt

1 dash of cloves

1 dash of pepper

3/4 tsp garlic

1/4 cup finely chopped onion

1/4 cup finely chopped celery

1/4 stick of cinnamon (remove before serving)

DIRECTIONS:

- In a food processor pulse the ginger into 1/8-inch pieces and set aside.
- In a food processor pulse mangoes into 1/2-inch pieces and set aside.
- In a sauce pan add onions, celery, ginger and garlic and allow to sweat.
- Once the vegetables begin to sweat add all the spices and stir for 1 minute.
- Add the rest of the ingredients and bring to a boil.
- Once the chutney hits boiling point reduce heat to a medium flame
- Let the chutney simmer and reduce until it is thick, about 30 minutes.
- Once the chutney has a thick consistency and looks like a chunky salsa you may serve it hot, warm or cold
- Yields about 2 cups

Chutney

SRIRACHA-HONEY BBQ

Vegetarian, Gluten-Free

This smoky, spicy topping is at its best with Duluth Grill barbecue sauce (you can find the recipe for that in the first cookbook). Use it for an extra kick on burgers.

INGREDIENTS:

1/2 cup Sriracha

1/2 cup barbecue sauce (DG homemade barbecue sauce preferred)

1/4 cup honey

2 tablespoons lime juice

DIRECTIONS:

- Whisk all ingredients together.
- Yield: 1.5 cups

Sriracha Aioli

SRIRACHA AIOLI

Vegetarian, Gluten-Free, Fast and Easy

Ok, let's admit it—aioli is mayonnaise. But aioli sounds a lot more sophisticated, doesn't it? Aioli is a French sommelier; mayo is a guy selling Bud Light. As a side note, imagine some poor first-grader trying to pronounce "Sriracha aioli" by sounding it out. Phonics isn't going to help you here, kid.

INGREDIENTS:

1 1/2 cups mayonnaise

1/4 cups sriracha

1 Tbsp dill

1 Tbsp lemon juice

1 tsp paprika

1 tsp onion powder

1 Tbsp minced garlic

DIRECTIONS:

- Blend all ingredients. Serve.
- Yields 1 1/2 cups

GREEN TOMATO JAM

Vegetarian,Vegan, Gluten-Free, Fast and Easy

One fall at the Duluth Grill, there were a few days were the only three jam choices were chokeberry, wild plum, or crab apple cardamom. But like these other choices, green tomato jam isn't just weird for weirdness' sake. It's got a compellingly spicy flavor that evokes Christmas puddings and Indian chutneys and a fun green color too.

INGREDIENTS:

1 1/2 lb quartered green tomatoes

2-inch piece of ginger

2 3/4 cups sugar

zest of 1 lemon

3 Tbsp lemon juice

1 2-inch cinnamon stick

1/2 tsp ground allspice

1 1/2 tsp salt

1/4 tsp cloves

DIRECTIONS:

- Zest the lemon and juice it. Combine all ingredients in a pot and bring to a boil. Reduce heat and let simmer until some caramelization occurs.
- Blend until smooth. Strain through a strainer, blend the strained pulp and stir into the jam.
- Yields 2 ½ cups

GREEN CHILE SALSA

Vegetarian, Vegan, Gluten-Free

Bermuda, Bahama… if the Beach Boys had had this salsa they might have sang a different tune. "Habanero, jalapeño, ooh I want to eat you. Cilantro, poblano, don't need no tomatoes." Roasting the peppers gives them a smoky flavor and reduces the heat.

INGREDIENTS:

1 lb tomatillos
1 jalapeño pepper
1 poblano pepper
2 habañero peppers
2 Tbsp chopped cilantro
1/4 cup Pico de Gallo
1 Tbsp water
4 2-ounce can green chiles
1 tsp garlic powder
½ tsp salt
1/8 tsp black pepper
1 Tbsp lime juice
2 Tbsp red wine vinegar

DIRECTIONS:

For Mash:

- Heat oven to 450°F
- Discard poblano pepper stems. Roast peppers on stovetop open flame and place into a bowl.
- Place tomatillos on a sheet tray with seeded and stemmed jalapeño and habanero peppers. Roast until golden brown.
- Place all ingredients into food processor and puree.

For salsa:

- Combine all ingredients with the mash into a large bowl and mix until fully incorporated. Serve.
- Yields 4 cups

Green Chile Salsa

CURRY SAUCE

Vegetarian, Vegan, Gluten-Free, Fast and Easy

Curry favor with your saucy friends with this vegan, gluten-free little number. The secret is in toasting the spices beforehand, a technique popular in India for bringing out deeper flavors.

INGREDIENTS:

1/4 cup seeded and stemmed serrano chiles
1 ½ tsp coriander seeds
1/4 tsp cumin
1/8 tsp black peppercorns
1/2 stalk lemongrass
1 tsp chopped cilantro
1 Tbsp grated fresh ginger
1/2 lime zest
1 tsp lime juice
1 Tbsp chopped garlic
1 Tbsp diced onion
1 ½ tsp aminos
2 Tbsp sugar
1 ½ tsp salt
1 ½ tsp turmeric
1 15-ounce can Thai coconut milk

DIRECTIONS:

- Toast coriander seeds and black peppercorns in a skillet. Trim and chop lemongrass. Combine all ingredients except coconut milk in a food processor until smooth.
- Place puree into a medium pot and simmer for 5 minutes.
- Add coconut milk, whisk, and simmer for another 15 minutes. Serve.
- Yields 2 cups

CILANTRO LIME VINAIGRETTE

Vegetarian, Vegan, Gluten-Free, Fast and Easy

This tangy, Latin-inflected vinaigrette is one of the first recipes people started asking for after the Volume One cookbook was printed.

INGREDIENTS:

2 Tbsp lime juice
1/2 cup cilantro
1/2 cup extra virgin olive oil
1/4 tsp salt
1/4 tsp white pepper
1/4 cup maple syrup
2 Tbsp cider vinegar
2 Tbsp orange juice
1 tsp brown mustard

DIRECTIONS:

- Combine all ingredients except olive oil in blender.
- Blend until smooth.
- Add olive oil slowly to emulsify.
- Yield: about 1½ cups

Cilantro Lime Vinaigrette

CAESAR DRESSING

Gluten-Free, Fast and Easy

Did you think Caesar salad was Italian, named after Julius Caesar or one of the other emperors? It was actually invented in the 1920s in Mexico. Because of Prohibition, Italian immigrant Caesar Cardini opened up a restaurant in Tijuana instead of San Diego. He ended up inventing the salad after running low on ingredients and making do with what he had.

INGREDIENTS:

1 cup mayonnaise
2 Tbsp apple cider vinegar
2 Tbsp grated parmesan cheese
1/2 tsp granulated garlic
1/2 tsp black pepper
1/2 tsp minced garlic
1 tsp anchovy paste
1 tsp brown mustard

DIRECTIONS:

- In a small mixing bowl, combine all ingredients.
- Yield: about 1½ cup (12 ounces)

Caesar Dressing

PORK RUB

Vegetarian, Vegan, Gluten-Free, Fast and Easy

Warming cumin gives this a taste of Mexico and the Middle East, and cayenne and black pepper add some heat. But the real secret is the touch of sage, which subtly invokes breakfast sausage.

INGREDIENTS:

1/4 cup salt
2 Tbsp paprika
2 Tbsp chili powder
2 Tbsp black pepper
2 Tbsp brown sugar
1 Tbsp cumin
1 Tbsp granulated garlic
1 scant teaspoon cayenne
1/2 tsp sage
1/4 tsp cinnamon

DIRECTIONS:

- Combine all ingredients and mix until fully incorporated. Store in an airtight container.
- Yield: about 1 cup

The Scoville rating

The level of ***Capsaicin*** *makes peppers hot. The Scoville scale (created in 1912 by American pharmacist Wilbur Scoville) measures this spiciness in Scoville heat units (SHU)*

SEASONED SALT

Vegetarian, Vegan, Gluten-Free, Fast and Easy

With almost no calories, this crunchy and easy vegan snack packs a serious flavor punch. Put it in a bowl for an easy breakfast, lunch, or dinner. Is eating a half-cup of seasoned salt with a spoon not your style? Stretch it out by sprinkling onto chips, fries, hash browns, or other fried foods.

INGREDIENTS:

4 Tbsp salt
1 Tbsp smoked paprika
1 Tbsp black pepper
1 Tbsp granulated garlic
1/2 tsp onion powder

DIRECTIONS:

- Combine all ingredients and mix until fully incorporated.
- Yield: about 1/2 cup

PICKLED JALAPEÑO

Vegetarian, Vegan, Gluten-Free, Fast and Easy

If there's a party in the Duluth Grill fridge every night, pickled jalapeños are the guys getting the conga line started. Fiery, tart, and sweet, these low-calorie gems bring life to every sandwich without putting anyone's dietary restrictions at risk in the process. As written this recipe is a refrigerator item and not shelf-stable, but you can make it shelf-stable if you know proper canning procedures.

INGREDIENTS:

1 pound jalapeño (about 20 large)

1/2 pound julienne onions (about 1 medium onion)

Brine:

3 cups cider vinegar

1 cup sugar

1 Tbsp yellow mustard seeds

1½ tsp turmeric

1½ tsp celery seed

1 tsp ground ginger

1 Tbsp salt

DIRECTIONS:

- Place ingredients for the brine in a large saucepan.
- Bring to a boil and let simmer for 5 minutes.
- Remove stems from the peppers and slice 1/8-inch thick.
- Place alternating layers of peppers and onions in a clean quart jar. Do not fill above the rim.
- Add the completed brine.
- Place lids on jars and process for 10 minutes in boiling water.
- Refrigerate, let sit for at least a week before opening.
- Yield: 3 pints

HABANERO CRANBERRY KETCHUP

Vegetarian, Vegan, Gluten-Free, Fast and Easy

The Duluth Grill has been making its own ketchup for years, but if there was one complaint the cooks heard time and time again, it's that there were no cranberries or habaneros in it. They solved the problem with this sweet and spicy variation.

INGREDIENTS:

1 1/3 cup ketchup

1 1/3 cup dried cranberries

1 habanero pepper, de-seeded

1/4 tsp salt

1 Tbsp plus 1 tsp red wine vinegar

DIRECTIONS:

- Place cranberries in hot water for 5 minutes to bloom the cranberry.
- Drain and add cranberries to blender.
- Remove stem from pepper and add to blender.
- Add the rest of the ingredients to the blender and blend until smooth.
- Refrigerate until ready to use.
- Yield: about 2 cups

FISH BRINE

Gluten-Free, Fast and Easy

This is the simplest and most delicious way to get moist, flavorful fish. If you haven't tried it, you simply have to. That's not a figure of speech—this fish is so good it's mandated by the Patriot Act. You've been warned.

INGREDIENTS:

4 cups water

3 Tbsp salt

1.5 Tbsp sugar

1 Tbsp lemon juice

DIRECTIONS:

- Add all ingredients to a small stock pot.
- Turn on high heat and dissolve sugar and salt (boiling is not necessary).
- Remove from heat and cool. Do not put fish in brine before brine is completely cooled.
- Yield: enough brine for 4 fish filets

RICE WINE VINAIGRETTE

Vegetarian, Vegan, Gluten-Free, Fast and Easy

Serve this with a salad of greens, Mandarin orange chunks and candied almonds for an light and Asian-inspired salad.

INGREDIENTS:

1 cup rice wine vinegar

1 cup extra virgin olive oil

1 tsp salt

1 tsp ground black pepper

DIRECTIONS:

- Put all ingredients in a blender and blend for about 10 seconds.
- Store in a shakable/pourable container (oil and vinegar will separate)
- Do NOT refrigerate! The oil will become very thick and will not mix.
- Yield: 2 cups

Habanero Cranberry Ketchup

Rice Wine Vinaigrette

BLUEBERRY SYRUP

Vegetarian, Vegan, Gluten-Free

The classic way to make blueberry syrup is to screw up making blueberry jam so that it doesn't set correctly. If you're aiming for syrup from the start, though, this recipe will get you there.

INGREDIENTS:

4 cups frozen blueberries (1 lb)

1 cup sugar

1 tablespoon pectin mixed with 6 tablespoons of water

DIRECTIONS:

- In a sauce pan, heat frozen blueberries on low heat until they release juices.
- Add sugar and stir.
- Let simmer for 10 minutes.
- Use spindle blender to puree.
- Prepare fruit pectin as per directions on box: make a slurry of pectin and water, and stir together over medium heat until it has boiled for 1 minute.
- Add 1 Tbsp of pectin mixture to the berries, stirring constantly for 3 minutes.
- Use spindle blender and mix again.
- Run syrup through strainer.
- Run excess pulp through blender (Vitamix if you have one) and mix back into syrup.
- Refrigerate unused syrup.
- Yield: about 2½ cups.

BLUEBERRY JAM

Vegetarian, Vegan, Gluten-Free

It's hard for out-of-staters to believe but Minnesotans do occasionally find themselves with too many fresh-picked blueberries. Jam is an easy way to preserve the season's bounty and can be made with frozen blueberries too if fresh are not available.

INGREDIENTS:

4 cups frozen blueberries

4 1/4 cup sugar

1 1.75-ounce box of fruit pectin (or 6 Tbsps of bulk pectin)

3/4 cup water

DIRECTIONS:

- In a saucepan, heat frozen blueberries on low heat until they release juices.
- Add sugar and stir.
- Keep on low heat and let set for 10 minutes.
- In another small saucepan, bring water and pectin to a boil, then stir for one minute longer.
- Add pectin mixture to the berries stirring constantly for 3 minutes.
- Either can the jam in a water bath or pour into a container and refrigerate.
- Yield: approximately 5 cups

APPLE BUTTER

Vegetarian, Vegan, Gluten Free

Apple butter is applesauce's muscular older brother, with a sweetness and intensity closer to a jam or jelly.

INGREDIENTS:

5 to 6 pounds of fresh apples

¾ cup apple juice

1/2 cup sugar

¼ cup brown sugar

1 tablespoon apple cider vinegar

1/8 cup lemon juice

1/4 tsp vanilla

1/4 tsp cinnamon

1/2 tsp salt

1/8 tsp nutmeg

1/8 tsp ginger

1/8 tsp ground clove

DIRECTIONS:

- Cook down 5 to 6 pounds of fresh apples. Cut into quarters and bring to a slow simmer. Cool.
- Strain out the seeds and stems through a china cap strainer as follows: using a small soup ladle, fill the strainer and with an up and down pushing motion push the apple through the strainer. The seeds, and stems will remain in the strainer and you end up with full apple pulp.
- Combine with rest of ingredients in a kettle.
- Cook on medium low heat for 1 hour.
- Yield: 6 cups

RASPBERRY SYRUP

Vegetarian, Vegan, Gluten-Free

Wild raspberries are one of the best parts of summer in Minnesota, and with this syrup, pancakes will never be the same again.

INGREDIENTS:

4 cups frozen raspberries

1 cup sugar

2 tsp fruit pectin

1/3 cup boiling water

DIRECTIONS:

- Start water boiling in a pan or teakettle.
- In a saucepan, heat frozen berries on low heat until they release their juices.
- Add sugar and stir, let sit for 10 minutes.
- In a heat resistant bowl, mix pectin and water thoroughly.
- When pectin has dissolved completely, add to raspberries and stir over medium heat for a few minutes.
- Serve right away, refrigerating leftovers or can using your favorite canning method.
- Yield: about 2½ cups

RASPBERRY JAM

Vegetarian, Vegan, Gluten-Free

Raspberries have vitamin C, vitamin K, and folate, along with antioxidants and polyphenols. More to the point, they taste like summer.

INGREDIENTS:

4 cups frozen Raspberries (about 1lb)

4 cups sugar

1 1.75-ounce box fruit pectin (or 6 table spoons of bulk fruit pectin)

3/4 cup water

DIRECTIONS:

- In saucepan heat frozen berries on low heat until they release their juices.
- Add sugar and stir.
- Let set for 10 minutes.
- In a second small saucepan, stir water and pectin until boiling, then stir 1 minute longer.
- Add pectin to berries, stirring constantly for 3 minutes.
- Cool and refrigerate or can using your favorite canning method.
- Yield: about 5 cups

TURKEY BRINE

Gluten-Free

If you're tired of dry turkey at Thanksgiving, try brining it next year. It's so moist and juicy you'll never look back.

INGREDIENTS:

1 gallon water
1 cup salt
3 bay leaves
2 Tbsp dry thyme
1 Tbsp dry sage
1/2 cup honey
1 thawed turkey

DIRECTIONS:

- Bring 1 quart water to a boil.
- Add the salt, honey, and spices and boil for 1 minute.
- Remove from heat and add 3 quarts very cold water.
- Put 1 turkey in a 5 gallon bucket and cover with brine. Use a dinner plate to keep the turkey submerged.
- Brine for 3 days.
- Bake turkey at 325°F until internal temperature reaches 165°F

Approximate cooking times by weight of turkey:

6–8 pounds: bake for 2½–3 hours
8–12 pounds: bake for 3–4 hours
12–16 pounds: bake for 4–5 hours
16–20 pounds: bake for 5–5½ hours
20–24 pounds: bake for 5½–6 hours

- After internal temperature reaches 165°F, remove the turkey from the oven and let it rest, covered for 30 minutes.
- Yield: 1 turkey.

TURKEY GRAVY Fast and Easy

Never made your own turkey gravy? If you're cooking the bird anyway, you'll definitely want to try this simple recipe. It's so simple and tasty you'll never want to use the packaged mix again.

INGREDIENTS:

Roux:

5–6 Tbsp butter

1/3 cup flour

Base:

(if you don't have turkey stock) 2 cups water

1 Tbsp chicken base

Pinch of ground sage

Pinch of seasoned salt

Pinch of dried parsley flakes

(if you do have turkey stock) 2 cups turkey stock with the fat removed

Pinch of ground sage

Pinch of seasoned salt

Pinch of dried parsley flakes

DIRECTIONS:

Roux:

- Bring butter to a slow boil on low heat.
- Add flour, stirring constantly.
- Once the roux is the consistency of wet sand, cook for 50 seconds to 1.5 minutes on medium heat.

Base:

- In a separate medium sauce pan, add base ingredients and bring to a boil.
- Once base has come to a boil, add roux.
- Return to a boil, stirring constantly.
- Reduce to simmer and cook until thickened.
- Yield: about 2½ cups

Turkey Gravy

BEET RAMEKINS

Vegetarian, Vegan, Gluten-Free

Impress your friends! Beets are sturdy and colorful, which makes them a great novelty container for salad dressings or sauces and you can eat them when you're done. The Duluth Grill has filled them with orange glaze to serve with a duck confit. To get the beet juice stains off your hands, use lemon juice and salt.

INGREDIENTS:

Whole roasted beets

DIRECTIONS:

- Cut stem and root off each beet.
- Peel skin off with paring knife.
- Cut in half (stem and root should be top and bottom).
- Place stem or root side down on cutting board.
- Use a tomato corer or spoon to hollow each half
(should look like a ramekin or bowl).

To roast beets:

- Preheat oven to 350°F
- Wrap beets with foil (should be air tight)
- Place on a baking pan and bake for 80-90 minutes or until tender
- Once beets have cooked, unwrap them to ensure rapid cooling
- Yield: 2 times as many bowls as beets you start with

A VISIT FROM THE FUTURE

THIS BLOG POST FROM 2014 TELLS THE STORY OF ONE OF THE SPOOKIEST GUESTS WE'VE EVER ENCOUNTERED. THERE'S A SIGNPOST UP AHEAD: YOUR NEXT STOP: THE TWILIGHT ZONE.

The other day we got a very unusual visit. Some of our older guests experienced ancient history (like the era where people talked to each other instead of their phones, or where gas was $1.50 a gallon), but until late July we've never met anyone from the future.

But all that changed. We got a comment card the other day from an anonymous guest who gave his name as "Fellow time traveler". The date of visit was Valentine's Day, 2048.

"We're from the future," he wrote in the comments section. "In 2038, this restaurant blew up. It was so famous that we had to come back in time to enjoy it."

The guest gave us 5 out of 5 in every area (food quality, menu variety, etc). Nostalgia may have played a role.

In 2038, this restaurant blew up. It was so famous that we had to come back in time to enjoy it."

DULUTH GRILL
DULUTH, MINNESOTA
Comment Card
Please Rate The Following
Food Quality Excellent (5) 4 3 2 1 Poor
Menu Variety Excellent (5) 4 3 2 1 Poor
Service Excellent (5) 4 3 2 1 Poor
Vibe Excellent (5) 4 3 2 1 Poor
Cleanliness Excellent (5) 4 3 2 1 Poor
Overall Experience Excellent (5) 4 3 2 1 Poor
Date of Visit 2/14/2048 Time 14:38 Server Name
Your Name Fellow time traveler Phone Number
Comments We're from the future. In 2038, This restaurant blew up. It was so famous that we had to come back in time to enjoy it.

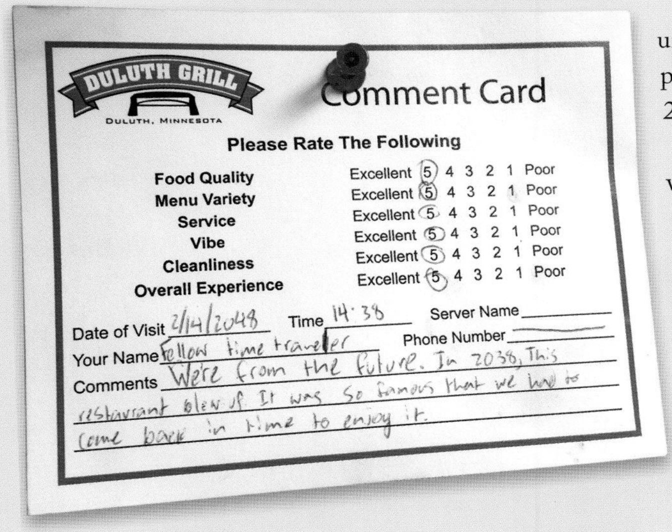

But wait, does nostalgia even apply if you actually visit the past instead of remembering it? There are other interesting questions this raises, too. The "phone number" field has a line through it. Does this mean that in the future we won't have phones? Or perhaps spending the money for a trip back in time left our visitor unable to afford the steep prices phone companies will charge in 2048.

At any rate, our future visitor was very kind, and it's helpful to get a handle on what's coming next. It will be sad when the restaurant is blown up someday, but at least now we can plan for it. Tom says we're officially listing the restaurant for sale in 2037.

"We didn't know where we'd be in the future," Jeff says, "but now we know!" **DG**

PROPOSED NAMES FOR THE SECOND BOOK

IT'S TOUGH TO DO A SEQUEL WELL. HERE ARE A FEW PROPOSED TITLES FOR THE SECOND COOKBOOK THAT ULTIMATELY DIDN'T MAKE THE CUT.

The Revenge of Duluth Grill
The Bride of Duluth Grill
Duluth Grill And The Last Crusade
Duluth Grill V: The Empire Strikes Back
Return to The Duluth Grill
Alien vs Predator vs Duluth Grill
Duluth Grill After Dark
Duluth Grill: The New Class
2 Duluth 2 Grill
Duluth Grill With A Vengeance
The Duluth Grill Ultimatum
Duluth Grill 2: Judgment Day
Duluth Grill and the Prisoner of Azkaban
Duluth Grill's Christmas Vacation
Duluth Grill vs. Godzilla
Cradle 2 The Grill

500 POUNDS OF PEPPERS

THIS BLOG POST FROM SEPTEMBER 2012 IS ONE OF THE GRILL'S MOST POPULAR

If you gave most people 500 pounds of fresh bell peppers, they would panic. At the Duluth Grill? Well, we still sort of panicked.

"When I walked into the cooler I was like 'whoa'," manager Jeff Petcoff said. "I felt like I was on an episode of *Hoarders*."

The story starts with UMD's farm on Riley Road, which has a good working relationship with the Duluth Grill. Probably spurred on by freeze warnings and, well, by having five hundred excess pounds of bell peppers, they dropped off one mega-shipment here last Friday and the other yesterday.

Kitchen staff were less than enthusiastic about winning the Pepper Powerball. But Tom, who has never met a vegetable he didn't like, thought of it more like green gold. He related a conversation he had with chef Dan, who he found staring mournfully at his newfound bounty.

"I said 'you look like you're pouting," Tom said. "Dan said 'it's total irresponsibility to have this much on

Hearing that one third of the world's food goes to waste is abstract. Having to deal with 500 pounds of peppers is personal.

hand.' I said, 'This is the opportunity of a lifetime. We could be typical and just dump it. Or we could push ourselves.'"

So we temporarily replaced onion rings with a new product—bell pepper rings. They're very good, like a mild, cheeseless-but-crunchy version of jalapeño poppers. Perhaps more importantly, the sudden shipment spurred a really interesting conversation about food production and responsibility.

Over beverages and bell pepper rings (well, at least I was eating bell pepper rings), we talked about whether or not it's kosher to be so haphazard about windfall produce.

"It IS close to being irresponsible," Tom admitted.

"It's irresponsible of them." Jaima responded more firmly.

Tom took another angle.

"No, it's not," he pondered. "It's like the grandma who gives you her old couch."

"But a little heads-up, maybe, that all this product is coming in?"

"We're kind of partnered with them."

"But a partner that doesn't communicate?"

"The communication was, 'sure, we'll take it.'"

"Well," Jaima said. "Ok then."

There was slight pause. Jaima took a sip of her smoothie.

"If it's worth nothing," Tom said finally, "It's worth a new blog this week."

Working with local farms definitely brings supply-and-demand issues a lot closer to home. Hearing that one third of the world's food goes to waste is abstract. Having to deal with 500 pounds of peppers is personal.

Ultimately, we're going to make the best of this situation. We'll use as much of the pepper haul as we can to prevent it from going to waste. And maybe we'll get something new out of the deal. As Tom points out, buffalo wings used to be considered a waste product before someone out in New York turned them into a major commodity. Now, they've become a popular menu item across the whole country.

"I'm not saying pepper rings will do that," Tom said.

"But they could," Jeff added. DG

1,700 POUNDS OF PEACHES

YEARS LATER, THE GRILL KEEPS ACCIDENTALLY GETTING WAY TOO MUCH PRODUCE

The phone rings—it's the Duluth Grill.

"Hey Robert," Jeff says. "Remember how two years ago we got 500 pounds of peppers?"

I did.

"Guess what we got this year?" Jeff continues. "2,000 pounds of peaches."

Santayana (the philosopher; not the guy who played Black Magic Woman) once said "Those who cannot remember the past are condemned to repeat it." And change happens fast. One day, you're at the top of the world with the three biggest weeks in the restaurant's history and a second cookbook on the way. The next, you're buried under a mountain of surprisingly juicy peaches. It was actually a little over 1,700 pounds, but probably felt like more to Jeff.

All day long, people had been coming up with recipes. Peach cobbler, peach salsa, peach soup. Peach pie, peach jam, peach syrup.

"What else?" Jeff asks.

A voice on the other end responds and Jeff parrots each answer back to me.

"Peach wine," the voice says. It sounds like Tom. That wouldn't surprise me; he's had his share of produce mishaps.

"Peach vinaigrette," the voice says. "Peach ice cream."

So how did the Grill end up with so many peaches? It's the kind of thing that makes you wonder. For that matter, how could ANYONE end up with that many peaches?

One day, you're at the top of the world with a second cookbook on the way. The next, you're buried under a mountain of surprisingly juicy peaches.

Catering manager Don Doane explains.

"On Sunday I had to run in and go shopping at Sam's Club, and out at the front door is Skyline Rotary selling their peaches. I was going to buy a case. They went 'Yeah, we bought 4 extra pallets and just went overboard. Would Duluth Grill take some?"

I said, 'I can look into it.'

So I take my case, I take the case for their dessert, and I leave. I can't get ahold of Lou. I say 'I'll call Tom'. I said 'Tom, they had four extra pallets and they were wondering if we'd take some.' Tom says, 'why don't you go back and tell them we'll take a pallet?'

I said ok.

Now, I don't know how big a pallet is. I roll down my window and say 'we'll take a pallet but you have to deliver it'. I should have known we were in trouble when we got a thumbs up like 'oh, you're a hero!'"

I came the next day and I swear the entire kitchen wants to shoot me. It was 80 cases of peaches in the refrigerator."

Wait. Did Tom know how much he was getting? Apparently not. Jeff says the peaches were measured not in pounds, but in pallets.

"I think Tom didn't realize how much a pallet was," Jeff says. "It ended up being close to a ton of peaches." DG

THE PEOPLE BEHIND THE FOOD
ALAKEF COFFEE

You knew the Duluth Grill grew herbs and produce, but did you know it grew all of its own coffee too? Well, it would if it was a little warmer outside. Something about "growing coffee" and "-20°F winters" doesn't exactly fit well together, and greenhouse heating costs would probably stretch the budget.

Rather than charge $11.95 a cup and grow it himself, though, Tom decided to go with an even better option. Local coffee roaster Alakef Coffee has been a Northland treasure since 1990 and passed on to its second generation in 2015. Owner Alyza Bohbot still remembers when her parents started the company in 1990.

"We recently added one sales person, otherwise our newest employee has been with us 6 years."

"I was pretty young," she says. "I was 6 I think. We'd sit at the kitchen table on weekends and put labels on bags."

But in the last 25 years, she and the company both grew up. In addition to Alyza and her parents, who are still involved, Alakef has nine full-time employees. The company picks just the right blend of coffee beans, roasts them, and delivers them the same day to the Duluth Grill's door.

Owner Alyza Bohbot

"We still roast to order on a daily basis," Alyza says. "Everything's still done very much by hand."

That kind of attitude makes for loyal customers. The Duluth Grill has been using Alakef coffee since 2007 and a bottomless cup of coffee is the top selling single item at the restaurant. But it also makes for loyal employees. Alakef pays well above minimum wage, offers full health and dental coverage, and a 401k profit-sharing plan. As a result, the average employee sticks around for years.

"We [recently] added one sales person," Alyza says. "Otherwise our newest employee has been with us six years."

Alakef isn't just concerned about its own employees, either. By buying fair trade and Rainforest Alliance certified coffees, the company makes sure workers abroad are paid a fair wage. The company's USDA Organic coffees, policy of recycling and composting, and focus on sustainable packaging mean it's taking care of the environment too.

The long story short is that when you buy a cup of coffee at the Duluth Grill, you're basically saving the world. Now that's something you can raise a glass to! DG

Beverages

COLD PRESS COFFEE

Vegetarian, Gluten-Free

Utterly smooth, highly caffeinated, and hard to stay away from once you've had it, this coffee drink will change the way you think about java. Note that this is a true concentrate and you will not want to drink it straight.

INGREDIENTS:

2 cups ground Alakef coffee

4 cups cold water

Any flavor that you enjoy (chocolate, caramel, vanilla) with milk, cream or whatever your heart desires!

DIRECTIONS:

- Mix together and cover for a minimum of 12 hours.
- Filter once through a strainer to get the grains out.
- Then, pour through a sieve with a coffee filter to strain again.
- Yield: 3–4 cups of concentrate

Cold Press Coffee

Iced Mocha-Nut

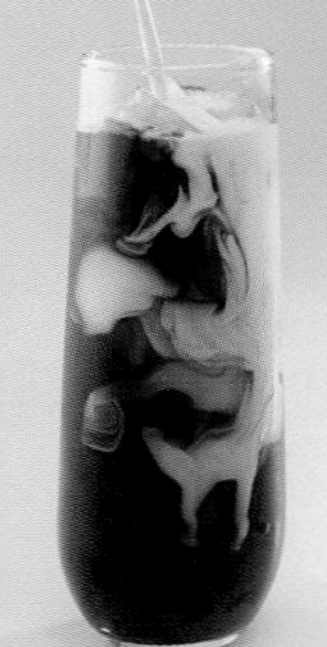
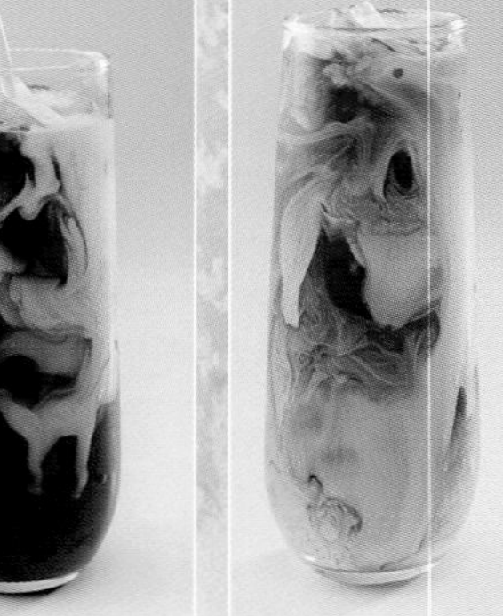

Mix in cream to taste and create your own lava lamp!

ICED MOCHA-NUT

Vegetarian, Gluten-Free, Fast and Easy

INGREDIENTS:

6-8 coffee ice cubes (frozen coffee in ice cube tray)

2-3 ounces chocolate sauce (reserve a little for topping)

1 cup vanilla coconut milk

1 ounce honey

whipped cream for topping

toasted coconut for topping

DIRECTIONS:

- Add all ingredients to a blender and blend until smooth.
- Pour in a fancy mug and top with whipped cream, chocolate sauce and toasted coconut.
- Yield: 1 serving.

VANILLA SYRUP

Vegetarian, Vegan, Gluten-Free, Fast and Easy

INGREDIENTS:

1 cup water

2 cups sugar

1/4 tsp cream of tartar

2 Tbsp vanilla extract

DIRECTIONS:

- Combine water, sugar, and cream of tartar in a sauce pan and bring to a simmer, stirring to help the sugar dissolve.
- Remove from heat, whisk in vanilla.
- Let cool.
- Yield: 1.5 cups

HOMEMADE LEMONADES

Vegetarian, Vegan, Gluten-Free, Fast and Easy

When life hands you lovage, make lemonade. No, wait. When life hands you beet juice, make lemonade. You know what? Old proverbs were a lot simpler before the Duluth Grill started getting fancy with their summer beverages.

INGREDIENTS:

12 ounces homemade lemonade

One of the following:

5–7 lovage leaves

5–7 mint leaves

1/2-ounce beet juice

One ounce of blueberries, blended

DIRECTIONS:

- Pour 2 ounces of lemonade in bottom of glass.
- Add 4-6 leaves (lovage or mint).
- Muddle together leaves and lemonade for 15 seconds, taking care not to over-muddle.
- Pour rest of lemonade into glass, fill with ice garnish and one additional leaf.
- Commence refreshment.

BEET:

Fill glass with lemonade.

Top with ice.

- Pour beet juice on top.
- Stir in and commence refreshment.
- Yield: 1 glass

Note: Muddling *is lightly crushing the leaves under liquid to release some of the flavor. You don't want to overdo it or the drink will be bitter.*

Lovage

Lovage is a wild herb with a mild celery flavor. You won't find it in stores but it's worth growing in your own garden because it adds a punch to soups and stews. The Germans call it "Maggikraut" ("Maggi herb") because it smells like Maggi sauce.

Beet Lemonade

Blueberry Lemonade

Mint Lemonade

WHERE DID ALL THE FISH GO?

The Long and Painful Process of Starting a Fish Farm

In fall 2014, the Duluth Grill had one of "those" weeks. By that time, they had spent the last few years very slowly trying to get an aquaponics system going. Tom and Jaima have a large greenhouse in their backyard which François uses to get a jump start on next season's planting. It's heated to a semi-reasonable temperature in the occasionally -20°F winter through a combination of solar heating and heat pumped in from the basement.

The centerpiece and master stroke of this greenhouse is the aquaponics system. There's a 4,800 gallon tank of water, and suspended above it hanging, porous, trays containing gravel and plants. Water circulates up from the fish tank and waters the plants. The plants filter out the fish waste, and at the same time the fish waste serves as fertilizer for the plants. Tom's goal was to grow a large school of pacu, a type of piranha that's vegetarian (no one wants to see the Hanson grandkids reach their tiny fingers into a tank of regular piranha).

> *"We started seeing a little bit of death," Tom says. "Then we started seeing the healthy ones float up. Then big pacu got sick. Then it became this rapid situation where the fish were just dying."*

It had been quite the learning process. So far, the team had learned that it was really expensive to heat 4,800 gallons of water. They had learned that it was not easy to haul hundreds of pounds of gravel. And they had learned that when you drop a wrench on the lower quality type fish tank liner, it causes a rip that's really hard to repair. But starting the fish part was also harder than they thought it would be. Here's what happened.

The Grill had one pacu in the restaurant in a fish tank, which was

named Pacu. He made friends with the youngest guests, who were just old enough to tap on the tank but not quite old enough to read the sign forbidding this. He also had a smaller sidekick fish named Al Muerzo (Spanish for "lunch"). Pacu grew to an enormous 24 inches. At 8 to 10 pounds he was too big for the restaurant's tank so they moved him back to the garden/aquaponics tank as their first resident. François put 35 new little pacu in the tank to join him and Tom noticed a curious problem.

Pacu, King of the Tank

"He wasn't eating any of his food," Tom says. "Then all of a sudden the fish we put in, it was like, where are they? So we assume he ate them all."

Oops.

So it turns out pacu aren't purely vegetarian after all (or that they're smart enough to rationalize cheating on their diets, which is even scarier). The gang at the Grill figured more robust pacu would perhaps avoid becoming prey. So they (the Grill staff) built a floating basket to protect them (the fish) until they (the fish, but possibly also some of the Grill staff) grew larger. Then they added 100 more. This little school of 150 pacu seemed about right, so they added 60 more.

"We started seeing a little bit of death," Tom says. "Then we started seeing the healthy ones float up. Then big pacu got sick. Then it became this rapid situation where the fish were just dying."

It turns out the new fish had been infected with a parasite. And then, as a result, the old ones got infected with that parasite.

By the time Tom's contact at the Great Lakes Aquarium identified the problem, added a 25 pound sack of salt, and stabilized the situation, they were down to perhaps 10 or 12 pacu.

Oops again.

There's a silver lining. The team at the Grill is learning to farm fish here, and every lesson counts.

"The valuable lesson of this is: we've advanced to now knowing that we have to quarantine all our fish," Tom says.

At the time the first cookbook was written (2012) the Grill was all about the fish. As of press time, and after a few more struggles like this one, the tank was down to zero. That doesn't mean there won't be a fish farm someday. But for now, management is considering simpler options.

"The fish, we're not 100% focused on," Jeff says. "We're kind of looking at rabbits." DG

THE PEOPLE BEHIND THE FOOD

NORTHERN HARVEST

One of the biggest challenges of sourcing local food is the supply chain. Frankly, the reason globalized agriculture spread so fast is that it's cheaper. Finding a location with the ideal climate for a particular vegetable and growing it on a large scale adds so much efficiency that produce from far away ends up less expensive than produce from nearby. And then there are the other advantages of centralizing multiple suppliers, like having one invoice instead of thirty and not having to worry about losing access when one farmer's crop fails.

But the globalized model also comes with huge trade-offs.

When agriculture is outsourced to other countries, there are no guarantees the workers are treated fairly. Human trafficking and slavery is especially prevalent in the fishing industry but all industries have their share of mistreated workers. Depending on the region food comes from, there may be lax oversight as far as the types of pesticides used or the safety

"Here people can say 'this food is coming from Wrenshall.' They can relate to that."

of the food handling. There's a certain environmental impact to all of the infrastructure used to carry produce across the world, whether that's exhaust from transport jets or just the oil used to make rubber truck tires.

Inside the US, federal and state oversight cut down on the worst of the labor offenses. But even so, large-scale, centralized agriculture has taken farming out of the hands of the small family farm and put it onto large corporations. Local farms allow communities to become self-sufficient and they can help restore trust in the food system. Because of this, the Duluth Grill sources almost 35% of its food products from around 30 local producers.

Rick and Karola Dalen own the Northern Harvest Farm in Wrenshall, Minnesota. Northern Harvest runs a popular CSA and sells to several restaurants, but Duluth Grill is one of its largest clients. For Rick Dalen, that volume has helped him build a business.

"They want to get things that are the bulk of their menu," Dalen says. "And the core of their menu they want to source them locally. So, they buy in quantity."

The Grill has purchased a lot of produce from Northern Harvest: kale, lettuce, cherry tomatoes, beets, cucumbers, and onions. The Wrenshall farm, which is around 25 miles from the Grill, is 34 acres—several acres in vegetables and soil building crops, an orchard that's on its way to production, and buffer/wild areas. While the farm uses a greenhouse to extend its growing season, Dalen's focus is on growing things in season rather than expending too much supplemental heat.

"If people want to move our food economy in a more sustainable way," Dalen says, "[They should] think about eating things in a sustainable way. Not expecting that they can eat anything any time of year, which is pretty much what we have gotten used to."

The farm is dealing with plenty of challenges, from the difficulty of competing with larger farms on price to the long hours inherent in the job. But Dalen believes that local food is the future. By growing things in a local, sustainable way, he's trying to bring back an ancient connection between a community and its farms.

"I think the big problem with big modern industrialized agriculture is people become disconnected with the land," Dalen says. "[Here] people can say 'this food is coming from Wrenshall.' They can relate to that." DG

PASSING THE TORCH

Letting go is hard to do.

Just ask Jaima Hanson. For the first few years she co-owned the Duluth Grill, Jaima made every dessert herself. The restaurant got so popular that she never quite seemed to be finished.

"If we would go on a vacation, I would be making cheesecake and chocolate cakes and everything so we could store it in the freezer," Jaima says. "And I'd be stressing out."

Finally, Tom stepped in with a question. Jaima still remembers the conversation.

"Jaima," Tom says. "What happens if you die, who's going to make all the desserts here?"

"Nobody eats dessert then anymore." Jaima says.

"You've gotta hand everything over," Tom says.

Years later, Jaima barely touches the cake mixer. The restaurant sees 1,000 guests a day during the summer and with over 100 employees, she's handed over the reins to a new generation of cooks.

"Everybody else can make it just as good or better than I could," Jaima says. "That's our end goal, to teach everybody else and pass it on."

The Hansons have owned the Duluth Grill since 2001. Since that time, they've grown gardens, become the highest rated restaurant in the city, and appeared on national TV. They've seen their children get married and become grandparents. And they've worked long days in the restaurant, week after week and month after month. Now, they're working on a new challenge—letting go.

For years, Tom has been trying to work himself off of the schedule. He keeps popping back in to work

Jaima, hard at work at her other job with Peyton and Parker.

"Jaima, what happens if you die, who's going to make all the desserts here?"
"Nobody eats dessert then anymore."

shifts, but gradually he and Jaima are taking more vacations. It's time, Jaima says, for the second generation to take over. Her son Louis Hanson, his best friend and honorary Hanson Jeff Petcoff, and Dan LeFebvre were typical high school punks when the Hansons took over the Grill. (Louis, for example, had this thing called the "Hanson hustle", where he would really ham up being injured in a hockey game to get the ref to call a penalty on the other team). But they've matured. Now, fourteen years later, they're top managers responsible for the welfare of a multimillion dollar organization.

"I'm very confident that we have Louis and Jeff and Dan to carry on the restaurant," Jaima says. "We're very fortunate to have those three behind us and with us."

Dan has been with the Grill for nine years and rose to become the head of the kitchen. He's responsible for food buying, menu development, and training in new chefs. He says he's excited to take on greater responsibilities and glad to see the restaurant moving forward.

"To see all the work and effort you've put into a business come to life is awesome," Dan says. "I think everybody's going to rise to the occasion."

Jaima, of course, has known Louis since the days when his primary interaction with the outside world was drooling on it. As a mother, she knows his weaknesses better than any outside manager could possibly hope to. But even so, she's proud of the job he does and has no doubt the three young leaders will carry the Duluth Grill's legacy.

"He's doing really good," Jaima says. "He still has a ways to go. There are a few detail things all of the guys need to recognize they're missing, but that will all come with time."

Her son Louis Hanson, his best friend and honorary Hanson Jeff Petcoff, and Dan LeFebvre were typical high school punks when the Hansons took over the Grill.

Dan says that this growth, and the learning curve involved in running a restaurant, are part of what make the process worth it.

"That's what's exciting, to push yourselves to higher levels," he says. "I think if we weren't to go in that direction it would get stagnant."

Tom and Jaima aren't going anywhere just yet. But they've started leaving on increasingly long trips. They'll make rare phone or email contact, but for the most part leave everything up to their staff. So far, things have been fine. No one's been hurt. Nothing's burned down. And the Duluth Grill hasn't landed on NBC nightly news for a series of sensational crimes.

Jaima says that she's confident that, in time, the new generation will prove to be worthy of the honor. But for now, she and Tom still can't resist keeping a finger on the pulse of the restaurant. She says her biggest challenge right now is "actually, really, letting go". She recognizes that she and Tom can't always be watching and keeping tabs, and the day will come when they have to completely turn things over.

But not today.

"I don't think they're ready for that one yet," Jaima says. DG

Jeff Petcoff, Dan LeFebvre and Louis Hanson

Breakfast

BISCUITS

Vegetarian, Fast and Easy

"*I like bread, and I like butter—but I like bread with butter best.*" Sarah Weiner's quote could apply to these biscuits, which have both butter and buttermilk right in the dough.

INGREDIENTS:

2 cups flour

1/4 tsp baking soda

1 Tbsp baking powder

1 tsp salt

6 Tbsp butter

1 cup buttermilk

DIRECTIONS:

- Butter or line a sheet pan with parchment paper and preheat the oven to 450°F.
- Cube butter and chill in refrigerator.
- Combine dry ingredients in a bowl.
- Add chilled butter to the flour and work mixture (a pastry blender works great) until butter chunks are crumbled, or about pea-sized.
- Add buttermilk and mix until just combined.
- Turn out the dough onto a lightly floured table.
- Pat dough into a 1/2-inch thick rectangle. Fold dough in half and pat to 1/2-inch thick rectangle.
- Repeat patting and folding five times to create flaky layers)
- Pat dough out to about 1-inch thickness.
- Cut out biscuits with a biscuit or cookie cutter.
- Line biscuits on sheet pan (for a tall, soft-sided biscuit, place dough close together. For a crustier biscuit, separate dough on the pan).
- Bake in oven for 10–15 minutes.
- Let cool and enjoy!
- Yield: about 16 biscuits

SCONES

Vegetarian, Fast and Easy

Scones are essentially biscuits with cream added. This gives them an additional richness, making them a perfect accompaniment for tea or coffee. Also, they are a good fit for the Grill since it's in *Minne-scone-ta*, next to *Wis-scone-sin*. We'll be here all week.

INGREDIENTS:

11 ounces (2 1/3 cup) all-purpose flour

2 ounces (4 Tbsp) cold butter

1 1/2 tsp baking powder

3/4 tsp salt

1/4 cup plus 1 Tbsp brown sugar

1 egg

3/4 tsp vanilla

1 cup heavy whipping cream

1 1/2 cup filler (chopped fruit, nuts, or chocolate chips)

DIRECTIONS:

- Cut the butter into 1/2-inch cubes.
- Combine baking powder, salt, brown sugar, and flour in a food processor. Add butter and blend until mixture resembles coarse sand.
- Transfer to a large mixing bowl. Whisk together egg, vanilla, and whipping cream and add to flour mixture. Gently combine. Stir in filler of choice. Do not over mix. Mixture should be dry in appearance.
- Turn onto a well-floured surface and press into a 1/2-inch thick disk. Cut into 8 wedges. Place wedges onto a lined sheet pan and bake at 350 for 20-25 minutes. Put on a rack to cool and serve.
- Yields 8 scones.

CHORIZO

Gluten-Free

According to conventional wisdom, you don't want to see how the sausages are made. But if you're using pure, natural ingredients, there's nothing to fear. A bit of heat complements the fattiness of the chorizo to make this even more addictive.

INGREDIENTS:

1 pound coarse ground pork

2 tsp salt

1/2 tsp ground black pepper

5 tsp ground *guajillo* pepper (you can buy whole *guajillo* and grind in food processor)

1 ½ tsp brown sugar

1 ½ tsp chopped fresh garlic

1 ½ tsp apple cider vinegar

1 ½ tsp dried oregano

DIRECTIONS:

- Combine all ingredients except pork in a mixing bowl and stir to combine thoroughly.
- Mix in pork either by hand, using your fingers to work in the seasoning, or with the paddle attachment on a mixer.
- Cover bowl and refrigerate overnight.
- Portion and cook or freeze for later use.
- Yield: 1 pound chorizo

BREAKFAST SAUSAGE

Gluten-Free

This breakfast sausage has the typical spices like sage and fennel, but wild rice gives it an unusual nuttiness.

INGREDIENTS:

1 Lb ground sausage

2 Tbsp sage

1/2 tsp salt

1/2 tsp black pepper

1/4 tsp dry marjoram

1/4 tsp dry oregano

1/2 tsp smoky paprika

1/2 tsp crushed red pepper

1/4 tsp fennel seeds

1 dash of cloves

1 dash of cinnamon

1/4 cup cooked wild rice

2 Tbsp maple syrup

1/3 cup water

DIRECTIONS:

Place all the spices and mix together thoroughly.

- Add water to the spices and stir until incorporated.
- Place sausage and all the ingredients in a large mixer and mix thoroughly (should take at least 5 minutes).
- Freeze, refrigerate or cook right away.
- Yields about 8 patties.

COUNTRY GRAVY

Country gravy, take me home, to the place, I belong.

John Denver never actually sang about this sauce, which gets its rich flavor from bacon grease and sausage drippings, but he should have. You could also put this on mashed potatoes, country fried steak, or fried chicken.

INGREDIENTS:

Roux

1/4 cup bacon grease

1/4 pound (1 stick) butter

1/2 cup all-purpose flour

Base

1 tsp chicken base

1 1/2 tsp black pepper

1 tsp sage

1 1/2 tsp salt

2 cups 2% milk

1 cup water

2 sausage patties

DIRECTIONS:

Dice sausage patties and brown sausage in a skillet.

- In a separate pot, add milk, water, black pepper, sage, salt, and chicken base and bring to a boil.
- Add browned sausage and drippings to pot.
- In a separate skillet, add butter and bacon fat and simmer over medium heat.
- Let butter melt, then add flour and cook for 2-4 minutes.
- Add roux to base and stir until the gravy thickens (this happens very quickly).
- Remove from heat and let cool.
- Yield: enough gravy for 16 biscuits

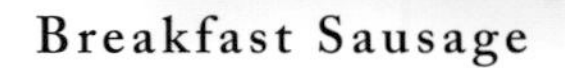

Breakfast Sausage

QUICHE

Vegetarian, Gluten-Free

2014 called, and it wants its quinoa, chia seeds, and Greek yogurt back. But trends become trends for a reason, and this brunch favorite is packed with great nutrition and taste. And do save the recipe, because in 30 years it will be the perfect retro party dish.

INGREDIENTS:

Crust:

3/4 cup quinoa

1/4 cup chia seeds

1 tsp curry powder

1/4 tsp salt

2 cups water

Filling:

5 eggs

2 egg yolks

1 cup Greek yogurt

1 tsp brown mustard

1 tsp turmeric

1/4 tsp cayenne

1/4 tsp salt

1 cup chopped broccoli (1/2-inch)

1/2 cup chopped scallions (1/4-inch) or 1/8 cup chopped fresh chives

1/4 cup nutritional yeast

DIRECTIONS:

Crust:

- Preheat oven to 350°F.
- Boil water in small stock pot.
- When water is boiling, add all ingredients.
- Mix until fully incorporated.
- Cover and reduce heat to a medium simmer for 8-10 minutes.
- Remove from heat and add to pie pan.
- Form a pie crust by gently pushing around the edges.
- Bake for 10 minutes.

Filling:

- Add eggs, egg yolks, Greek yogurt, mustard, turmeric, cayenne, and salt to mixing bowl and whisk until fully incorporated.
- Fold broccoli and scallions or chives into liquid mixture.
- Place baked crust on a sheet pan.
- Distribute nutritional yeast evenly over the baked crust.
- Pour egg mixture on top of yeast.
- Bake in oven at 350°F for 30–35 minutes or until internal temperature reaches 140°F.
- Yield: One pie pan

BUCKWHEAT CARAWAY BREAD

Vegetarian, Gluten-Free

If you're looking for something hearty and gluten free, this is the perfect choice. This bread works well for camping since it packs a lot of nutrition, fills you up, and doesn't take up much space (but put it in a Ziploc bag because it does tend to crumble).

INGREDIENTS:

1/2 cup vegetable oil

1/2 cup honey

3 eggs plus 1 egg for egg wash

15 ounce can of pumpkin

2½ cups buckwheat flour

1½ tsp chia seeds

1/2 tsp sea salt

1 Tbsp caraway seeds

3 tsp xanthan gum (helps hold gluten free breads together)

1/4 cup shelled sunflower seeds

1/3 cup shelled pumpkin seeds

2/3 hot water plus 2 Tbsp cold water for egg wash

1½ tsp baking soda

Black pepper, sea salt and sesame seeds for topping the bread

DIRECTIONS:

- Preheat oven to 350°F.
- In mixer, combine oil, honey, eggs, pumpkin, buckwheat, chia seeds, salt, caraway seeds, xanthan gum, sunflower seeds and pumpkin seeds on high for several minutes until well mixed. Batter will be thick.
- In a separate bowl, add baking soda to hot water, dissolve and add to batter on low.
- Mix until well combined, but not too long (batter will be very thick and sticky).
- Pour batter into greased bread pan (Note: once seasoned, stoneware pans need not be greased)
- Thoroughly mix 1 egg with 2 Tbsp of water and brush on loaf .
- Top with black pepper, sea salt and sesame seeds.
- Bake at 350°F for 60-75 minutes. Check with a toothpick to make sure loaf bakes all the way through.
- Let loaf sit in pan for about 10 minutes, then remove and place on cooling rack.
- Leave on cooling rack until thoroughly cool.
- Yield: 1 loaf

Note:

You MUST make sure to get shelled pumpkin seeds, the bread will not be very nice with unshelled pumpkin seeds.

BESAN CHILLA (VEGAN OMELET)

Vegetarian, Vegan, Gluten-Free, Fast and Easy

After Tom came up with a recipe for a vegan omelet, a gentleman from India tried it. "This is just like a chilla!" he exclaimed. "What's a 'chilla'?" Tom wondered. He looked it up and discovered it was a type of salty north Indian pancake made of garbanzo beans. And that's the story of how the Duluth Grill independently discovered the chilla (albeit thousands of years after it was first invented).

INGREDIENTS:

4 cups garbanzo bean flour
3 cups water
2 tsp turmeric
2 tsp onion powder
2 tsp white pepper
1 tsp sea salt
1 tsp garlic powder
3/4 cup diced onion (divided)
1 Tbsp fresh garlic puree
Oil (for the skillet)

DIRECTIONS:

- Place all ingredients except 1/2 cup diced onion to the blender.
- Blend until smooth.
- Transfer to a mixing bowl, add the rest of the onions, and stir to combine.
- Place a skillet over medium high heat.
- Lightly oil the skillet, then add batter to the pan and cook as if they were pancakes.
- Yield: about 4 large pancakes.

The Duluth Grill fills its chillas with corn, beans, red peppers, onions, and scallions, but feel free to fill with your favorite omelet filling.

BLUEBERRY MUFFINS

Vegetarian

One good rule of thumb is that everyone likes the guy who brings the blueberry muffins. Be that guy.

INGREDIENTS:

Muffins

2½ cups all-purpose flour

1 cup sugar

3/4 tsp salt

1 Tbsp baking powder

1/2 cup vegetable oil

2 eggs

1/2 cup milk

1½ cups frozen blueberries

Topping:

1/2 cup sugar

1/3 cup all-purpose flour

1/4 cup cubed unsalted butter

1/2 Tbsp ground cinnamon

DIRECTIONS:

- Line muffin tin with muffin liners.
- Combine oil, eggs, and milk in bowl, mix.
- Add in sugar and mix on high.
- Combine flour, salt and baking powder in another container and add to first bowl, mix well.
- Fold in blueberries.
- In a separate bowl, combine the topping ingredients and whisk together.
- Spoon mixture into muffin liners, about 3/4 full.
- Bake for 15-20 minutes at 350°F, check for doneness using a tooth pick.
- Yield: about 18 medium sized muffins

CHICKEN DREDGE AND MARINADE

Frying chicken often involves egg washes and complex batters. This simple dredge is an easy alternative.

INGREDIENTS:

2–3 pounds chicken breasts (skins or not, up to you)

Chicken Dredge
1/2 cup all-purpose flour

1 1/2 tsp seasoned salt

1 1/2 tsp black pepper

pinch of cayenne pepper

Chicken Marinade
1 cup buttermilk

1 Tbsp Tabasco sauce

DIRECTIONS:

- Trim chicken breasts and slice each breast in half, so that each portion weighs 3–4 ounces.
- Place chicken in a 9x13 pan and add marinade.
- Cover, place in refrigerator, and let sit overnight.
- Remove from the marinade, shake off excess liquid, and dredge each piece.
- Pan fry in at least one inch of oil (cast iron skillet is best) or deep fry over medium heat (about 5 minutes per side) and enjoy!
- Yield: about 12 portions, or 4 servings as a main course

TOM HAS AN AUCTION PROBLEM

How We Started Serving Vegan Ice Cream

We added homemade vegan ice cream to our menu last week. It's creamy and sweet, with a gentle key lime tang and hints of mango. But—as usual—the story behind it is the best part.

"[It's] homemade, from scratch," manager Louis Hanson begins—

"Made from a vision Louis had," fellow manager Jeff Petcoff adds.

Those two are like an old married couple. But Louis isn't finished yet.

"...while cursing Tom for buying an ice cream machine," Louis explains. "and realizing we had to do *something* with it."

Indeed, this year's been dubbed "The Year of the Auction". As the owner of the Duluth Grill, Tom Hanson has both vision for the future and access to the company credit card. That's a potent mix—sort of like gunpowder and a spark. Here's a small sample of this year's purchases:

1) Twenty racks for glasses
2) An Aunt Jemima rag doll
3) A sixteen-foot hood system that took four people to unload from the truck
4) Many, many antique lamps
5) An old metal scuba diving helmet a la Jacques Cousteau
6) Not one, but two paella pans. For thirty.

"You could sled down a hill with a friend in that thing," Jeff says.

But back to the ice cream. One of Tom's many auction acquisitions was an ice cream maker, and its first official contribution to our menu is the Avocado-Coconut Sorbet. With fresh, creamy avocado and coconut milk for a base, it has the same rich mouth-feel of a dairy dessert. Key lime and mango give it a tropical flavor. You may not be able to fly to Cancun this winter, but at least you can taste it from here.

People are responding well to the $3.50 dish, and

One of Tom's many auction acquisitions was an ice cream maker, and its first official contribution to our menu is the Avocado-Coconut Sorbet.

brainstorming is under way for new ice cream flavors. Future vegan options may include a straightforward coconut sorbet, and we're looking at adding regular ice cream too. Flavors under consideration range from vanilla to bacon maple to cardamom and local apricots. With so many options, the future is open wide—and there's no telling what creative flavors will ultimately make the cut.

"It's hard to say," Louis says. "We can do whatever we want." DG

**This blog post from early 2013 shows that everyone has a place in this world, and Tom's place is to get weird stuff at auctions and figure out a use for it later.*

UNDERDOGS UNITE

Proud to Be In Lincoln Park

You've seen the movie a dozen times. It starts at a summer camp or a dance studio or a community center. It's a little run-down and small-time, but for the quirky but lovable campers/dancers/neighborhood kids, it's home. Then a big, evil corporation wants to buy the property. Oh no! The only way to save it is for the scrappy underdogs to band together and win some sort of a contest against a team from the Big Rival Group. There's tension and drama, but at the end, they manage to save the community.

It's a little like that for the Lincoln Park neighborhood. But in this case, there's no big scary developer coming in. Duluth Grill and the other local businesses are the scrappy underdogs, and they're facing an altogether tougher battle. For years, the industrial neighborhood has been viewed as the "wrong side of the tracks". Now, though, a team of businesses is reinventing the community as a hip place to be.

Take the Bent Paddle Brewing Company as an example. The business is in its second year but already at the ninth year of its development plan. Last year it produced 7,850 barrels of beer and as of this writing was on track to produce 17,000 in 2015. The four owners, Karen and Bryon Tonnis and Colin and Laura Mullen, are passionate about the neighborhood.

"We were saying it's kind of like a northeast Minneapolis," Karen says. "Local, artisan, crafters…"

Karen and Laura are both involved in *Advancing Lincoln Park*, an organization campaigning to get the buzz going for the area. They're considering requesting grants, facilitating businesses to do economic development, and encouraging worthy businesses to open second locations in the area.

For years, the industrial neighborhood has been viewed as the "wrong side of the tracks". Now, though, a team of businesses is reinventing the community as a hip place to be.

"[It's] a neat way to get on board with this artisan economic area," Laura says.

Another neighbor making waves nationally is Frost River. The young Duluth company fell dormant in 2008, but when Christian Benson tried to buy a piece of equipment for his upstart leather mitten company, he was offered the whole brand. He bought Frost River, revived it, and moved it to a new building in Lincoln Park. Marketing director David Hoole

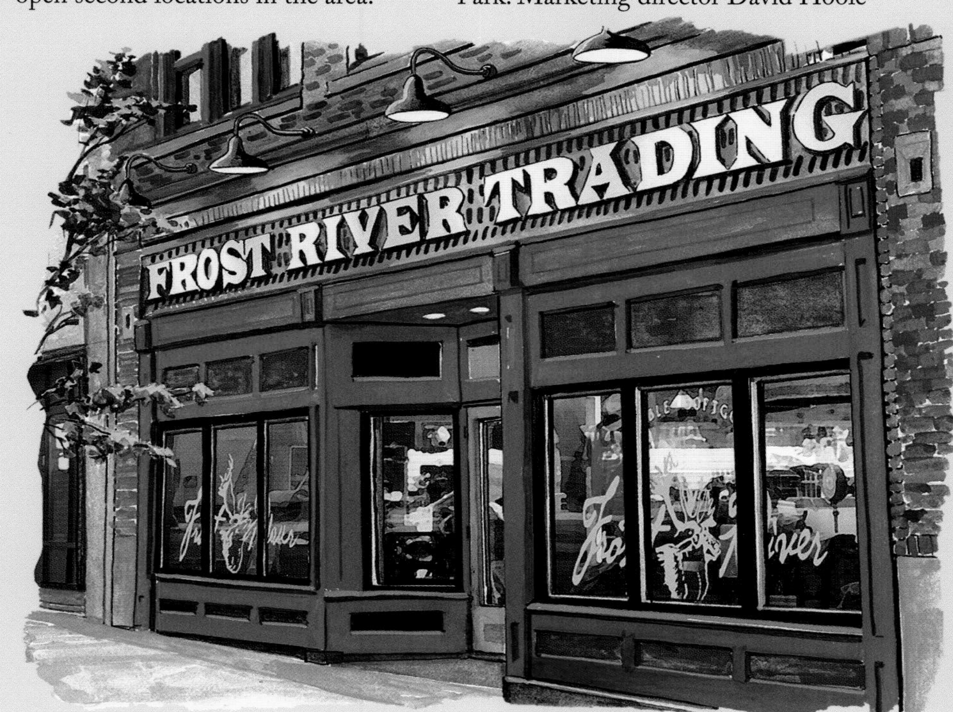

"I really feel that if we continue to invest in the community, the community is going to invest in us. These people are our partners and we all have the same goal and passion which is to really make this the hip-happenin' place to be."

says he's proud of the brand, which sells its leather and canvas canoe packs nationwide.

"I like that it's honest," David says. "It's fun stuff to talk about and easy stuff for people to see the value in."

Manufacturing seems to be the theme of the new Lincoln Park. From Epicurean, which manufactures high-end cutting boards, to Loll designs, which makes outdoor furniture from recycled milk jugs, the area is increasingly vibrant.

And it continues to grow. Benson bought another building next to Frost River, which has hosted local "pop-up shops" displaying businesses that have either moved to Lincoln Park or are considering the area. From Birchaus Market, a mobile lifestyle shop focused on unique Duluth designs, to Hemlocks Leather Works, which makes hand-crafted leather shoes, there's a lot of creative energy.

After years and years of bad memories of its first foray into a second location (an ill fated diner in Superior) even the Duluth Grill is getting in on the growth. The OMC, which stands for "oink, moo, cluck" will be a meat-focused barbecue place. Rather than getting swamped in debt, Tom's decided to bootstrap the new opening and could be found clearing away rubble or sweeping the floor through most of the build-out.

The food business is expanding in the neighborhood too. Duluth's Best Bread, a company the cookbook author totally started with his brother (and is totally writing about anyway as though he were objective), is just four blocks up the street from the Grill churning out crusty sourdough bread and flaky French croissants. Even more significantly, the Whole Foods Co-op is constructing a second location in the neighborhood to combat the area's status as a food desert.

Jeff says he sees Lincoln Park as a truly up-and- coming neighborhood and is excited for what the next ten years could bring

"I look at the future of where this is going," Jeff says. "I really feel that if we continue to invest in the community, the community is going to invest in us. These people are our partners and we all have the same goal and passion which is to really make this the hip-happenin' place to be." **DG**

Soups & Starters

PEANUT SOUP

Vegetarian, Vegan, Gluten-Free

Peanut soup is an African staple, especially when made with sweet potatoes, ginger and spicy pepper. This version brings in coconut milk for additional creaminess and cilantro for a fresh bite.

INGREDIENTS:

2 Tbsp olive oil

1 cup diced onion

1 Tbsp minced garlic

1/2 cup celery

4 cups diced sweet potatoes

2 13.5-ounce cans Thai coconut milk

2 13.5-ounce cans fire roasted tomatoes

1 cup peanuts

1 ½ tsp salt

1/4 tsp black pepper

1 ½ tsp coriander

1/2 tsp cayenne pepper

1 ½ tsp turmeric

2 Tbsp vegetable base

4 cups water

1 cup ginger root

1/2 cup chopped cilantro

DIRECTIONS:

- Peel and dice sweet potatoes and ginger root, but keep separate.
- Add oil to a large saucepan and sauté onions, garlic, and celery over medium high heat.
- Add sweet potatoes, coconut milk, and fire roasted tomatoes and reduce to medium heat.
- Mix vegetable base into 4 cups of hot water.
- Puree peanuts, salt, black pepper, coriander, cayenne, and turmeric and 1 cup of vegetable stock, and add this to the soup.
- Puree ginger root and 1 cup of vegetable stock, and add this to the soup.
- Add remaining vegetable stock.
- Add chopped cilantro to soup and mix until fully incorporated.
- Cook until sweet potatoes are tender.
- Yield: about 7 cups

Capsicum annuum:

The red pepper is a healthy choice. It's got tons of dietary fiber, Vitamin A, Vitamin C, and Vitamin E (Alpha Tocopherol).

PUMPKIN SOUP

Vegetarian, Vegan, Gluten-Free

Pumpkin pie's a nice thing to eat at Thanksgiving but you have to be pretty bold to serve it for dinner (at least more than once or twice a month). Split the difference with this unusual soup, which offers the cinnamon and nutmeg flavors you're looking for without the raised eyebrows from your dietician spouse.

INGREDIENTS:

1 15-ounce can pumpkin puree

3 cups vegetable stock

1/2 cup heavy cream

1/2 tsp cinnamon

1/8 tsp nutmeg

1/8 tsp white pepper

1/4 tsp cayenne

1/2 tsp salt

2 Tbsp orange juice

DIRECTIONS:

- Combine all ingredients in a pot.
- Whisk over medium heat until smooth. Simmer for 30 minutes.
- Puree and strain though a fine mesh strainer. Puree pulp and mix into soup. Serve.
- Yields 5 cups

SANGUINE MARIA SOUP

Vegetarian, Vegan, Gluten-Free

Get it? Like "bloody Mary"? If you look into a mirror at midnight and say "sanguine Maria" three times, a personal trainer appears and warns you to lay off the Frosted Flakes.

INGREDIENTS:

1 Tbsp olive oil

4 cups diced fresh onion (about 4 medium onions)

1 ½ tsp pureed garlic (about 3 cloves)

4 cups tomato filets (about 6 medium tomatoes)

1 quart tomato juice

1 cup pico de gallo

1 stalk diced lovage or celery

1 Tbsp dill

1/2 tsp white pepper

1 Tbsp Tabasco Sauce

1 tsp sugar

1/4 cup chopped lovage or celery leaf

1/2 cup diced kalamata olives

1/3 cup key lime juice

DIRECTIONS:

- Add olive oil to a small pan over very low heat. Add onions and garlic along with a dash of salt. Sweat onions until they are translucent, stirring often.
- Remove onions and garlic from heat and place in blender with the tomato fillets. Blend until smooth.
- Return ingredients to kettle, turn on low heat and add all the rest of the ingredients except for 1/2 cup of the pico de gallo.
- Simmer for 40 minutes without bringing to a boil.
- Remove from heat, add remaining cup of pico de gallo.
- Chill in an ice bath or the refrigerator.
- This soup is meant to be eaten chilled.
- Yield: 3 quarts

ZUCCHINI MINESTRONE

Vegetarian, Vegan, Gluten-Free

Zucchini grows so bountifully that you'll never get rid of it all in zucchini bread. Here's the rare recipe that makes this humble vegetable shine again. Thyme and sage, along with carrots, celery, and onion, make this a warming vegan accompaniment to any winter meal.

INGREDIENTS:

4 cups zucchini puree (recipe page 61)

1 Tbsp vegetable base

1 cup cooked garbanzo beans

1 cup diced carrots

1 cup diced celery

1 cup diced onion

1 cup diced zucchini

3/4 tsp thyme

1/2 tsp sage

DIRECTIONS:

- Place all ingredients in a large stock pot over medium high heat.
- Bring to a boil, then lower heat and simmer for an hour.
- Yield: about 6 cups

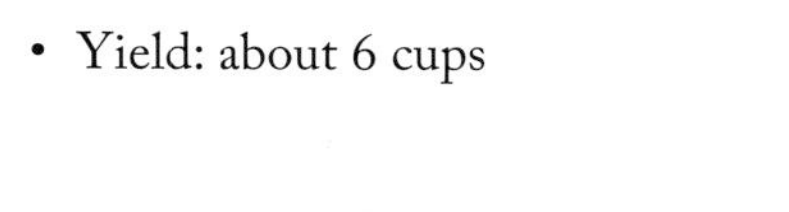

ZUCCHINI PUREE

Vegetarian, Vegan, Gluten-Free, Fast and Easy

Primarily used as a base for zucchini minestrone, this puree can also be doctored up with ricotta cheese and salt to make a mellow pasta sauce, or stir some into mashed potatoes for a way to get your kids to eat their vegetables. Or add olive oil, pureed pine nuts, and salt for a thin pesto-style sauce.

INGREDIENTS:

1 medium onion

1/4 cup chopped garlic cloves

3 pounds zucchini

1 cup packed basil leaves

DIRECTIONS:

- Dice the onion.
- Peel the zucchini and cut off the ends.
- Add all of the ingredients to a large pot
- Cook over medium heat until tender, about 15 minutes.
- Transfer ingredients to a blender and puree the mixture.
- Strain the puree through a fine mesh strainer.
- Add any chunks to the blender and blend until smooth.
- Add puree from the blender to the strained puree.
- Yield: about 4 cups

FISH STOCK

Gluten-Free

Use this as a base for fish chowders or any kind of seafood dish.

INGREDIENTS:

1/2 lb fish trimmings (bones or heads)

1/2 cup diced onion

1/4 cup chopped carrot

1/4 cup chopped celery

1/4 bay leaf

1/2 tsp rice wine vinegar

8 cups water

DIRECTIONS:

Add all ingredients to a large stock pot.

Simmer for 45 minutes.

Strain stock through a mesh strainer.

Discard vegetables and fish trimmings.

Yield: about 8 cups

BROCCOLI CHEESE SOUP

Vegetarian, Gluten-Free

If you'd like to get kids to eat their vegetables, you could do a lot worse than broccoli cheese soup. This creamy treat, which also works with cauliflower or summer squash, is made a little more elegant with Gouda cheese.

INGREDIENTS:

4 cups vegetable stock

2/3 cup diced white onion (one small onion)

1 cup fresh cut broccoli (or cauliflower)

1 pint heavy cream

1/3 cup corn starch

1/2 tsp white pepper

1/2 cup shredded Gouda cheese plus another 1/2 cup for sprinkling

2 1/2 Tbsp parsley flakes

1/2 tsp sea salt

DIRECTIONS:

- In stock pot, combine vegetable stock, onion, white pepper, salt and broccoli (or cauliflower).
- Bring to a boil.
- In a mixing bowl, combine heavy cream and cornstarch.
- Add cream and cornstarch mixture to boiling soup, stirring constantly.
- Reduce heat to a simmer.
- Add cheese slowly and stir until cheese is melted.
- When cheese is melted, add parsley flakes.
- Sprinkle remaining Gouda on each bowl, serve hot.
- Yields: about 6 cups

CHEESY HAM AND POTATO SOUP

Gluten-Free

Potatoes are the anchor for this creamy, smoky soup, which you can fine-tune with different kinds of cheese such as mild or sharp cheddars, jack, or even gouda or gruyere.

INGREDIENTS:

2 Tbsp olive oil

3/4 cup diced onion

4½ cups finely diced (or about 4 medium) potatoes

1 cup finely diced ham

1/2 tsp white pepper

1/2 tsp salt

6 cups vegetable stock

2 cups heavy cream

3/4 cup shredded cheese (you can vary the kinds, but cheddar is the classic)

1/2 cup corn starch

1 Tbsp parsley

DIRECTIONS:

- Saute onions in olive oil until translucent.
- In 4 quart pot add diced potatoes, sauteed onion, vegetable stock, ham, white pepper and salt.
- Bring to a boil, boil until potatoes are soft.
- In a mixing bowl, mix heavy cream and cornstarch.
- Add cream and cornstarch mixture to boiling soup, stirring constantly.
- Reduce to a simmer and slowly add the cheese.
- Add parsley flakes.
- Serve hot, refrigerate leftovers.
- Yield: about 12 cups

SPRING ROLLS

Vegetarian, Vegan, Gluten-Free

Fair warning: this recipe presumes you have marinated kale and carrot daikon slaw handy.

When the Duluth Grill grew way more mint one season than they had planned for, the chefs starting thinking of where else they could cram it on the menu. That led to a delicious lamb dish, mint lemonade, and also these unique spring rolls. If you're having trouble folding these without the paper ripping, use two sheets at once.

INGREDIENTS:

1/2 cup cooked wild rice

1 cup carrot daikon slaw (recipe page 83)

60 mint leaves (about a cup)

90 cilantro leaves (about a cup)

1 cup marinated kale (recipe page 89)

2 sliced (1/4-inch by 3-inch) roasted red peppers

1 head of bibb lettuce or butter lettuce

rice papers

warm water

Each spring roll will contain:

1 tsp cooked wild rice

1 Tbsp carrot daikon slaw

4 mint leaves

6 cilantro leaves

1 Tbsp marinated kale

1 slice (1/4-inch by 3-inch) roasted red peppers

2 leaves Bibb lettuce or butter lettuce

1 rice paper

DIRECTIONS:

Prep work:

- Finely chop marinated kale with food processor.
- Transfer to a strainer and press out any excess liquid.
- Set aside in a bowl for assembly.
- Fill a 9x13 pan with warm water, set up next to rice papers for assembly.

Assembly:

- Start by placing 1 rice paper in water bath (should not be in water for more than 20 seconds.)
- Place soaked rice paper so that the texture side is facing up.
- Build in order: bibb lettuce, wild rice, carrot-daikon slaw, mint leaves, cilantro leaves, kale, roasted red pepper.
- Fold sides in and tightly roll (should be 4-inches in length.)
- Yield: about 15 spring rolls

KALE & WHITE BEAN SOUP

Vegetarian, Vegan, Gluten-Free

Every piece of kale is like a venue holding a meeting of the Nutrients Club—iron, fiber, omega-3 fatty acids, and others gather around and exchange tips on keeping you healthy. With protein from white beans and vitamins from the cabbage, carrots, and rutabaga, this lean vegan soup is your secret health weapon.

INGREDIENTS:

1 cup diced onion

2 cloves minced garlic

1 cup dry white beans or 1 can cooked white beans

2 cups chopped cabbage

5 cups vegetable stock

1 cup diced carrots

1/2 cup diced rutabaga

2 cups chopped raw kale

1/4 tsp seasoned salt

1/2 tsp salt

1/4 tsp white pepper

1 Tbsp olive oil

1 tsp parsley flakes

DIRECTIONS:

- If using dry beans, cook until tender and drain.
- In a heavy bottomed stock pot, heat olive oil and cook down onions and garlic until tender, about 5 minutes.
- Add all other ingredients except parsley and cook until tender, for 1 hour.
- Add parsley flakes and serve. Adjust salt to taste.
- Yield: 8 cups

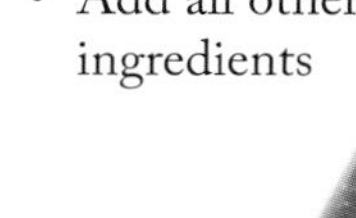

Jokes About Kale

What is kale's favorite state? ***Kale-ifornia.***

What is kale's favorite part of Michigan? ***Kale-amazoo.***

What is kale's favorite Blondie song? ***Kale Me***

What Supreme Court judge likes kale the best? ***S-kale-ia.***

What did Napoleon Dynamite have that would impress vegan girls? ***S-kales.***

WHITEFISH CHOWDER

Gluten-Free

Chowder has a long and storied history. Originally considered a poor man's food and made with leftover scraps, it gradually evolved into the soup we know today. While there are many theories as to which style of chowder is the most authentic (tomato based or cream based), we're writing the cookbook and we're going to go with "our version is". That should settle that.

Kale & White Bean Soup

INGREDIENTS:

1/4 cup diced onion

4 Tbsp butter

1 cup fish stock (recipe page 61)

1–2 cups of whitefish

1/4 tsp granulated garlic

1 tsp onion powder

1/4 tsp white pepper

1/4 tsp salt

4 1/2 cups 1/2-inch cubed potatoes (testers used Klondike Rose with great results)

6 cups water

1 1/2 Tbsp chicken base

1/2 cup corn starch

2 cups heavy cream

1 1/2 Tbsp parsley flakes

DIRECTIONS:

- In a sauté pan, sauté onion with butter.
- In at least a 4 quart pot combine whitefish, onion, potatoes, spices, water and chicken base.
- Bring to a boil, boil until potatoes are no longer crunchy.
- In a mixing bowl, mix heavy cream with cornstarch.
- Add to the boiling soup to thicken, simmer until chowder has thickened.
- Add parsley flakes.
- Serve hot, refrigerate leftovers.
- Yields: approximately 10 cups

TOMATO BRUSCHETTA

Vegetarian, Gluten-Free, Fast and Easy

A friend once praised someone's cooking ability by saying "she can make anything taste like pizza". While that's not always a positive it's certainly a plus for this quick appetizer.

INGREDIENTS:

Toast:

6-8 ciabatta rolls (ciabatta bread can have lots of air pockets that create holes, you can also try something more dense)

1/2 cup olive oil

1/2 tsp dried basil

1/2 tsp dried oregano

1/4 tsp salt

A pinch of white pepper

5-ounce container of shredded Parmesan

Bruschetta:

2 cups small diced deseeded tomatoes, finely diced

1/2 cup red onion, diced to 1/8-inch

1/2 ounce chiffonade (shredded) fresh basil

1 Tbsp balsamic vinegar

1/2 tsp minced garlic

1/2 tsp salt

DIRECTIONS:

- Preheat oven to 350°F.
- Cut ciabatta bread approximately 1/2-inch thick.
- Mix oil, basil, oregano, salt and pepper in small bowl.
- Lay bread on baking sheet (testers put down parchment paper) and brush with oil mixture.
- Sprinkle shredded Parmesan on bread.
- Bake for 5-10 minutes or until tops are like a crouton (testers liked it not quite so crunchy).
- Toss all bruschetta ingredients in a bowl.
- Drain excess liquid right before topping toast.
- Top toast with small amount of bruschetta mixture and serve immediately.
- Yield: about 3 cups Bruschetta mixture

Enlarge your culinary vocabulary!

"Chiffonade" means to shred. Stack some of your basil leaves on top of one another, with the stems all facing the same direction. Now roll them vertical to the stem and thinly slice the roll. This process can be used for many larger leaf herbs.

Chiffonade is a great word to wow your friends with and makes you sound like you really know what you are doing!

HUMMUS WITH PRESERVED LEMON

Vegetarian, Vegan, Gluten-Free, Fast and Easy

Preserving lemons in salt mellows them and turns them into a sort of "lemon pickle". This popular North African condiment makes for a nuanced raw hummus.

INGREDIENTS:

1 cup chick peas with liquid

1.25 ounces preserved lemon (about 2 wedges)

1/4 cup tahini

2 tablespoons olive oil

1 tablespoon miso paste

1/2 tablespoon minced garlic

pinch cayenne pepper

DIRECTIONS:

- Strain chick peas, preserving the liquid
- Blend all ingredients in a food processor, adding preserved chick pea liquid until mixture reaches a smooth, creamy texture.
- Yield: 1.5 cups

ALMOND FLAX CRACKER

Vegetarian, Vegan, Gluten Free

This is a raw recipe with all the crunch of conventionally baked crackers and a lot more flavor. These crackers keep a long time when kept in a dry environment.

INGREDIENTS:

1 1/4 cup flax seed (soaked 2–4 hours)

1 1/4 cup almonds (soaked 10–12 hours)

12 ounces sweet corn

1 cup diced red peppers (seeded and 1/2-inch dice)

2 tablespoons diced green pepper

3 tablespoons onion powder

4 teaspoons dry oregano

1 tablespoon cumin

1/4–1/2 tsp salt (to your liking)

1 cup water

DIRECTIONS:

- Drain and rinse the almonds, drain the flax.
- In food processor add soaked almonds and water and chop finely.
- Place everything in a large mixing bowl mix thoroughly
- Once everything is mixed together blend all ingredients into a batter. (A spindle blender is best for this. If you use a regular blender only blend small quantities at a time.)
- Place 2 1/2 cups of batter on a Teflon sheet and spread out evenly to about 1/4-inch thickness all the way to the edges. You'll want the equivalent of two and a half dehydrator trays so square up the half sheet to only be half of the tray.
- Place dehydrator for 2 hours at 115 degrees.
- After 2 hours, or after chips are at least dry enough to score with a pizza cutter, take sheets off of trays, score chips 4x4, then score on a diagonal to give you 32 chips. (They'll be easy to break apart when they're completely dry).
- Place in the dehydrator for 12 hours at 115 degrees.
- After twelve hours flip onto grid sheet.
- Place back in the dehydrator until cracker is crispy (about 6–8 additional hours).
- Yield: You should yield two and a half trays on a dehydrator with a total of 80 crackers. (32 per tray)

Note on Flax Crackers

Flax seeds and almonds will expand during the soaking process: make sure to use all flax and almonds in the recipe. There should be nothing left over.

THE PEOPLE BEHIND THE FOOD
ANAHATA HERBALS

The Duluth Grill sells both "hot chocolate" and "hot chagalate", so imagine the look on your young son's face when he learns that he accidentally ordered a cup of tea. Now imagine those concerned little eyebrows raising in delight as he takes his first sip.

That's because hot chagalate definitely has a chocolate flavor, with rich notes of cacao. But it's also loaded with chaga, a boreal mushroom that has a succulent, earthy flavor and more antioxidants than acai, blueberry, or pomegranate. With burdock, rose hips, a few other herbs, and stevia for natural sweetness, this tastes great with neither calories nor caffeine. In fact, go ahead and re-order for your kid. You'll be finishing this pot yourself.

Anahata Herbals is run by Eric Ament. The business originally started in 2010 when he met his wife, an acupuncturist who was working with a handful of traditional Chinese herbs. They rented a room and increased their assortment from 20 to 300 herbs.

"We started off as just a distributor," Eric says. "As we were distributing we'd also gather local plants. We bought six acres on the edge of town so we could grow more."

"How do I compete with these countries where people are getting paid $2 a day to harvest?"

He began supplying teas to companies around Minnesota. While he used to have some accounts in Minneapolis, he let most of them go, since he wanted to focus on the Duluth-Superior area. Scorekeeper, put another point in the Duluth column!

"In my mind I'd love to just stick to the Superior basin and focus on taking care of the people around here," Eric says.

But the tea business is hard work. If you've ever gone out and picked, say, wild blueberries, you know it takes a preposterous amount of time to harvest tiny little quantities. Some wild ingredients are even worse. Of course, Eric is better than you are at harvesting (no offense), but he's still only got two hands.

"You're spending four hours to harvest and you're lucky to get a couple of pounds," Eric says. "That is a big challenge. How do I compete with these large scale well developed farms in countries where people are getting paid $2 a day to harvest?

In a nutshell, that's the challenge the whole small-scale agriculture movement faces. The Duluth Grill has managed to hit a niche where customers are willing to pay a little bit more, but a lot of factors play into that—service, homemade food, and maybe most importantly, the "splurge factor" where people pay more to eat out. In retail, convincing people to pay more for local food is a tricky operation. Eric says he originally wanted to keep all sales local but had to broaden his net to make it work financially.

"I played around with the idea if I did online sales I'd only allow certain zip codes and keep it to local," Eric says. "And then the realities of bills come in."

Eric has been selling retail tea for years, but the Duluth Grill was his first restaurant account. He says that's given him boldness to continue and approach other restaurants. Now he is making around 30 different blends of tea. The Backcountry Blend is harvested 100% locally and is made with labrador tea, sweet gale, cedar, rose hips, sumac berries, and raspberry leaf. Others are made with a blend of local and out-of-town ingredients.

Tea is a labor-intensive business, and between three children and a wife with her own business, Eric says he often works late. But ultimately, he's doing this because it's something he believes in.

"The money comes and goes, sometimes it's great and sometimes it's slow," Eric says. "You just find a way." DG

KICKSTARTING A GARDEN

RAISING $18,811 ONE DONATION AT A TIME

Tom's "hypothetical" ideas are about as hypothetical as when your wife asks, "what would you think of visiting my family this year for Christmas instead of your family?" They may happen sooner and they may happen later, but rest assured, they will happen. So when Tom started talking in early 2013 about "maybe" "thinking" it would be cool "if" we ripped up the back parking lot, built a huge orchard, and oh by the way funded the entire thing with donations from the public, I started to brace myself.

But the project itself was important one. For the past two years the Duluth Grill had been working to expand the relevance of local food and at the same time help define urban agriculture in the city of Duluth. These projects started with large raised beds along the perimeter of the parking lot and grew to include containers in the front of the restaurant, a roof garden, and the front and back yards of Tom's house being full of plants.

The extensive back parking lot: there was a lot of wasted space. Frankly, it wasn't exactly the most attractive thing to look at.

That process made the team at the Grill look at the extensive back parking lot, where there was a lot of wasted space used neither for cars nor for planting. Frankly, it wasn't exactly the most attractive thing to look at. The team was also deeply concerned about designated trout stream Miller Creek, which runs behind the property. 900,000 gallons of runoff was flowing from the roof and parking lot into that stream per year (Tom made François stand out there whenever it rained to count each gallon as it went by).

Miller Creek is one of the many streams at the headwaters of the Laurentian watershed, its waters feed-

The hugelbed begins..

ing the chain of the Great Lakes, the world's largest body of fresh water. Running directly into Lake Superior the waters of the creek will eventually reach the Atlantic Ocean, sending along whatever pollutants and trash it picked up. This trash, plastics in particular, feeds the "Atlantic Ocean Garbage Patch" and the recently discovered Lake Erie patch.

Even today, the creek condition is rough. A group of students came to the restaurant to look at the gardens and actually watched the fish spawning among garbage.

"It's really obvious," Tom says. "They were like 'eww, ish, there's oil and shoes and cans.' I've gotten a little conditioned to it, [but] François was like 'look at that petroleum'. We kind of thought we'd better do something about it."

This just goes to show the importance of taking steps to solve the problem. By separating two rows of vehicles François figured he could open an area 140 feet long and 12 feet wide in the back lot and turn it into a cultivable tract. This orchard could provide fresh, natural food for the restaurant, beautify a blighted site, and mitigate the runoff all at once.

The specific project was a 140 feet long, 12 feet wide and 6 feet high berm following the permaculture technique of *hugelkutur*. The first step in a *hugelkutur* project is a pile of logs with dirt heaped over it. As the logs rot, they automatically till the soil and provide it with nutrients, as well as store and hold moisture, so the bed would sustain itself with little cultivation needed for decades.

But first we had to fund it. That meant going online and drumming up support through Kickstarter, an online fundraising site. The community was amazingly supportive and ended up

François begins the planting

contributing $13,811. It's crazy what a town will do when it puts its mind to something, and so to each and every person who contributed we say: thank you again.

Kickstarter lets you offer rewards, all the way from our sincere thanks at lower dollar levels to getting the garden named after you at the top. Getting into the pseudo-retail business like that had a few snags of its own. Starting at $1000 we were offering free admission to our three-day permaculture workshop, including room and board. We kind of dodged a bullet there since if anyone had picked that, we would have had to organize and host a three-day permaculture workshop. As it stands, the highest backers paid $500—the perfect mixture of a) generosity and b) us not having to host a big event.

My favorite part of the rewards process was thinking up the names, starting at "Seedling" and "Sprout" and going all the way through "Garden of Eden" and "The Legend". My least favorite part of the rewards process was figuring out who got what, tracking down their addresses, and making sure everything got sorted out. (Also, realizing that one of the reward options was lunch with me, and no one chose it.) But that's nothing in comparison to the long suffering Jeff Petcoff, who once a year or so switches from general

Once you get into the mold of asking people for money, it's actually kind of fun.

manager to a one-man order fulfillment house. With two years standing between us and that project, I figured it might be safe to ask Jeff how he felt about it.

"I'm not going to go there," Jeff says. But he didn't throw a fork at me for asking, which is progress of a sort. That isn't to say he's thrown forks in the past, either, but Louis recalls the days where it was a realistic threat.

"I'd peek around the corner and look at him like… 'I think he's doing good'," Louis says. "I was just staying out of it at that point."

Once you get into the mold of asking people for money, it's actually kind of fun. We had a meeting with fellow Lincoln Park neighbors at Mielke Electric that somehow ended with me and the owner's daughter talking in German and a large check. But probably the craziest and most heart-stopping moment came when we were talking to the wonderful Melody Fontaine. Melody is great with advertising and had talked to her longstanding clients Hartels/DBJ. Hartels does the Grill's waste removal and was flexible when the team wanted to start composting. She had gotten them intrigued with donating to the hugelbed. Now, the only question was how much they would give.

"So," I said, fishing around. "Ballpark, what were you guys thinking?"

"Maybe something like $3,000," Melody said.

That was a really generous offer. A REALLY generous offer. But this was a big project.

"Yeah, so, I would actually think in terms of $5,000," I said.

Time stopped for a moment. Out of the corner of my eye, I saw Jeff and Tom staring at me like I had sprouted cow horns. Did I just counter an offer of free money with a request for a HIGHER amount of free money?

"Of course, we'd be thrilled with any amount you can give!" I squeaked.

But for the rest of the conversation, I referred to the grant as "the full $5,000." Melody continued to smile. Hartels came through with $5,000 and presented it as a huge check, and we're thankful to this day.

It wasn't easy to dig out the garden, put the rocks down, or plant it. François spent countless hours getting the work done. But after months of effort, the back parking lot has been transformed. Between rows of cars, there's a forest garden with unique fruit and nut trees, vines such as kiwis, shrubs, perennial herbs, and edible flowers. It is open to the public as an educational piece where people can learn about both the ideas behind urban gardening generally and about our local ecosystem specifically.

It also became clear that there were more people willing to donate. The *Hobart Center for Foodservice Sustainability* awarded the Grill a $5,000 grant and said they beat out universities and even a small national restaurant chain. St. Louis County offered the Grill $8,000 to do further work, and while it wasn't a good fit at the time, it was a sign that the Grill was on the right track.

Aside from providing produce for the kitchen, beautification for the neighborhood, a habitat for wildlife, and a natural classroom for the community, the garden will help restore the pristine state of Miller Creek and the Great Lakes. The next stage in the process may be to build a rain garden, a network of drain tiles set in trenches crisscrossing the parking lot. It's a big job, but because of the community, it's one that's in reach. DG

ALL IN THE FAMILY

Baking With Jaima Hanson

Everyone's grandma makes the best cookies. Everyone's grandma makes the best cake. This truth is self-evident, on par with the rights to life, liberty, and the pursuit of happiness. But just like the animals in Animal Farm, all grandmas are equal—but some are more equal than others. This is partly luck, a matter of being at the right place at the right time. But it's also partly because some grandma recipes are too good not to be shared.

Take manager Louis Hanson's grandma, for example. Jaima Hanson learned to bake from her mother, and her cakes and cookies became the foundation of the Duluth Grill's dessert menu. Now, hundreds of thousands of people per year enjoy those old family recipes. And it all started with a little girl in a raspberry patch.

Your grandma might make the best cookies, but Jaima (who is now a grandma herself) makes a pretty fair substitute. And when grandma's not around, the Duluth Grill is still open

"I watched my mom bake all the time," Jaima says. "I was always in the kitchen with her. We had big rhubarb patches, big raspberry patches. I was always helping pick that."

Jaima's mother taught her to make pies, bars, cookies, and other treats. It's an influence Tom didn't exactly have at home.

"When I first met Tom, I was over there for Thanksgiving dinner," Jaima says. "I wanted to bring stuff. They said 'she's got it.' After

From left to right: Grandma Jaima Hanson, Peyton Hanson, Parker Hanson, mom Ashley Hanson.

Thanksgiving dinner was done, I said 'Let's do the next event at my house'."

Jaima has high standards when it comes to dessert. When she and Tom bought the Embers that later became the Duluth Grill, she didn't compromise.

"They did these icky crusts and they sent these big cans of strawberry glaze," Jaima says. "It was terrible. I remember I was serving a customer once, and the strawberry glaze stained that tabletop for a year."

She began to bake her own strawberry pies, but like the War on Drugs, the War on Terrible Premade Desserts wouldn't be easy to win. A year or so after Glazegate, Jaima encountered a new enemy—frozen cheesecake."I was cutting it up one day and thought 'this is just awful'," Jaima says. "I thought 'I can make my own cheesecake.'"

Cheesecake she learned from cookbooks, chocolate cake she brought from home. A s'mores ice cream cake finished with a blowtorch she made up. (She also introduced the velvet pumpkin cakes you'll find on page 124).

It all goes back to the mom factor. Your grandma might make the best cookies, but Jaima (who is now a grandma herself) makes a pretty fair substitute. And when grandma's not around, the Duluth Grill is still open, still making cake, still holding that coffee warm for you. Jaima's mother is currently staying with the Hansons, and who knows… maybe she'll influence the menu more directly.

"She should actually be at this restaurant," Jaima says. "She's got a palate, she bakes like nobody's business. She's really good." **DG**

Jaima with her baking instructor and mother, Darlyne Jansen

Cheesecake she learned from cookbooks, chocolate cake she brought from home. A s'mores ice cream cake finished with a blowtorch she made up.

Parker prepares to take over for his grandma… someday.

Sides

ITALIAN SAUSAGE

Gluten-Free

In medieval times, if you killed a pig in winter you could freeze the meat in the snow. But the rest of the year? Sausage is a traditional (and tasty) food preservation method that let people enjoy meat all year long. This version is meant to be kept in the fridge, but with 11 different spices, it's got as much complex flavor as the old styles. You can put this in lasagna, pasties, soup, peppers, or ravioli, make meatballs out of it, fry it with onions and green peppers and put it on a roll, or eat it plain.

INGREDIENTS

1.25 pounds ground pork

2 1/2 tsp salt

1 tsp fennel seed

1/4 tsp ground black pepper

1 tsp oregano

1 tsp crushed red pepper

1 1/2 tsp chopped fresh parsley

1 1/2 tsp red wine vinegar

1/2 tsp dried basil

1 tsp chopped fresh garlic

1/2 tsp dried thyme

1/2 tsp onion powder

DIRECTIONS:

- Combine all ingredients except pork in a mixing bowl and stir to combine thoroughly.
- Mix in pork either by hand, using your fingers to work in the seasoning, or with the paddle attachment on a mixer.
- Cover bowl and refrigerate overnight.
- Portion and cook or freeze for later use.
- Yield: 1.25 pounds sausage

VEGAN KIMCHI

Vegetarian, Vegan, Gluten-Free

Fermented foods like Korean kimchi are rich in probiotics, which are the same beneficial bacteria that colonize the gut. Pungent, salty, crunchy, and spicy, this side dish is worth waiting for.

INGREDIENTS

1 small head Napa cabbage (about 1.25 lbs)

3/4 cup shredded carrot

1 1/2 cup shredded red cabbage

1 1/4 teaspoon salt

Seasoning:

1/2 cup roasted red pepper

1 tablespoon minced garlic

1 tablespoon minced ginger

1 tablespoon minced green onions

2 teaspoons red pepper flakes

2 teaspoons agave

DIRECTIONS:

- Shred the Napa cabbage and add salt to the bowl.
- Massage the salt into the cabbage thoroughly and let sit: water will be released to make the brine.
- Combine all seasoning ingredients in a food processor until it forms a paste.
- Toss shredded carrots and shredded red cabbage together with the Napa cabbage.
- Work the paste into the cabbage with your hand (wear a glove!).
- Transfer into a 1 qt mason jar.
- Let sit 2–3 days, burping (release gas) once a day.
- After 3 days, place in the fridge.
- Yield: 1 quart

SAUERKRAUT

Vegetarian, Vegan, Gluten-Free

Most people think of sauerkraut as a German dish (after all, the name simply means "sour cabbage" in German). But while it's popular in Germany, it likely originated further east. Laborers working on the Great Wall of China were eating cabbage pickled in rice wine and some think Genghis Khan brought it to Europe during his invasions. See, more proof that sauerkraut makes you tough.

INGREDIENTS

2 large heads of cabbage (about 7 lb)

4 Tbsp salt

4 tsp caraway seed

1 1/2 tsp celery seed

1 bay leaf

Sauerkraut

DIRECTIONS:

- Quarter the cabbage.
- Shred the cabbage using a food processor, a cabbage shredder or cut into thin strips with a knife.
- Combine salt, caraway and celery seed with the shredded cabbage.
- Knead the cabbage mixture until water starts to come out.
- In a 1 gallon bucket or crock, add one half of the cabbage and pack it down.
- Add the bay leaf.
- Add into the bucket the rest of the cabbage and pack down.
- Pour in any liquid from kneading and pack down.
- Weigh down the cabbage with dinner plates or a freezer bag filled with water.
- Allow to sit at room temperature for 10-14 days.
- When it tastes like sauerkraut, it is done.
- Store finished kraut in the refrigerator.
- Yield: about one gallon

CARROT-DAIKON SLAW

Vegetarian, Vegan, Gluten-Free, Fast and Easy

Cabbage is usually the star of coleslaw, but daikon is a fresh and mild Asian vegetable that does just as well in the role. Give the understudy a chance in the limelight with this simple, crunchy, and healthy side dish.

INGREDIENTS

1/2 cup sugar

1/2 cup apple cider vinegar

2 cups shredded carrot (use cheese grater)

2 cups shredded daikon radish (use cheese grater)

DIRECTIONS:

- In a small sauce pot heat cider vinegar and sugar together until dissolved.
- Using the large size cheese grater run carrots and daikon radish over it and place in a sealable container.
- Place vinegar mix over the top and seal.
- Yields About 4 servings

Where to find preserved lemons? Try your local whole foods store or Middle Eastern market. Can't find them premade? There are several recipes online, but note they take a few weeks to make.

GREEN BEAN CASSEROLE

Vegetarian, Gluten-Free

Do you really need canned soup to make a green bean casserole? Wait! Don't turn the page; no one said anything about lightening this up. We're just saying wine, sherry, mushrooms, and cream might be an alternative route you could take to Delicious City.

INGREDIENTS

1 cup sliced mushrooms

2 Tbsp marsala wine

2 Tbsp cream sherry

1/3 cup heavy cream

1/2 tsp oregano

1/4 tsp white pepper

1/4 tsp salt

2 Tbsp cornstach

1/4 Tbsp olive oil

1 lb (one bag) green beans

DIRECTIONS:

- Sauté the mushrooms and salt in the olive oil until mushrooms have turned golden brown, about 5 minutes. Stir occasionally.
- Add the wine and sherry, allow the alcohol to boil off for 2-3 minutes.
- Add remaining seasonings and stir, bring to a simmer.
- Combine remaining 1½ Tbsp cream and cornstarch, stir to smooth consistency and add to the sauce, stir sauce constantly.
- Bring to a boil and remove from the heat.
- Steam green beans in steamer for 10 minutes.
- Rinse and cool green beans.
- Combine mushroom sauce with green beans and fold until combined.
- Serve immediately.
- Yields about 4 servings

Cream of Mushroom Soup

Several decades ago, many home cooks got their recipes from recipe pamphlets, which major food companies would produce as a way of encouraging people to buy their products. Green bean casserole goes back to 1955, when the Campbell's Soup Company's Dorcas Reilly thought of it as a way to drive sales of cream of mushroom soup.

WALNUT TACO MEAT

Vegetarian, Vegan, Gluten-Free

Walnuts themselves have a relatively neutral flavor but between fresh herbs, dried herbs, and savory miso paste this "taco meat" packs a punch. Serve these in lettuce wraps with fresh salsa (like pineapple salsa on page 16), guacamole, and cashew sour cream (page 15) for a raw vegan Mexican fiesta.

INGREDIENTS

1 cup raw walnuts, soaked 10–12 hours

1/3 cup pinenuts, not soaked

3 tablespoons deseeded, diced tomato meat

3 tablespoons frozen or fresh corn

3 tablespoons chopped green onions

4 teaspoons minced cilantro

4 teaspoons minced basil

4 teaspoons miso paste

2 teaspoons chili powder

1 teaspoon cumin

pinch salt

DIRECTIONS:

- Pulse walnuts and pine nuts in a food processor until coarsely ground.
- Add veggies, seasoning, and nuts in a mixing bowl and mix until fully incorporated.
- Yield: about 2 cups

EGG SALAD

Vegetarian, Gluten-Free, Fast and Easy

Detective Oeuf took a long draw from his cigarette and stepped out onto the rainy, crime-ridden streets. After a sleepless night, he knew who the killer was, and he'd do whatever it took to stop him.

INGREDIENTS

12 eggs, as hard-boiled as Detective Oeuf

1/2 cup finely chopped celery

1/2 cup finely chopped onion (red onions add color)

1/2 tsp salt

1/4 tsp pepper

1/4 cup chopped cilantro

1 Tbsp mustard

1/3 cup mayonnaise

DIRECTIONS:

- In this detective story, you play the villain. Peel shells from eggs, dice up and place in medium bowl.
- Add rest of ingredients and mix. You fiend. Watch out—Detective Oeuf's partner will stop at nothing to track you down.
- Serves 4-6

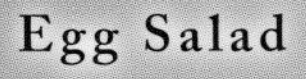

Egg Salad

WILD RICE PATTY

Gluten-Free, Vegetarian, Fast and Easy

There once was a nice girl named Patricia. But after she became a teenager, she joined a motorcycle gang and started eating only rice. This dish, the "Wild Rice Patty", is named after her.

INGREDIENTS

1 tsp white pepper

1 tsp salt

1 ½ tsp granulated garlic

4 ½ tsp cumin

1 ½ tsp crushed red pepper

1 cup crushed gluten free Chex

1 ½ cup mayo

4 eggs

1 cup diced mushrooms

5 cups cooked wild rice

DIRECTIONS:

- Preheat oven to 350°F.
- Mix white pepper, salt, granulated garlic, cumin and crushed red pepper together in a large mixing bowl.
- Add remaining ingredients and mix well.
- Measure mixture into 8-ounce (1 cup) portions and form into patties.
- Place on baking sheet and bake for 30-35 minutes.
- Yield: 7 patties

BACON-BLUE CHEESE COLESLAW

Gluten-Free

With an indulgent creaminess from bacon, blue cheese, and real mayonnaise, you'll be shocked to learn that this side dish is actually diet friendly. Well, assuming you have a very lenient diet.

INGREDIENTS

1 cup mayo

1/3 cup bacon fat

1/3 cup finely chopped cooked bacon

1/3 cup apple cider vinegar

2 Tbsp sugar

1/2 tsp celery seed

1 tsp salt

1/2 tsp pepper

1 small head finely chopped green cabbage

1/3 lb shredded carrots

4 ounces blue cheese

DIRECTIONS:

- Cut cabbage into quarters and slice to make thin strips.
- Cut the ends off the carrots and run them over a cheese grater.
- Chop bacon into 1/4" pieces and cook in sauté pan to ensure bacon is crisp.
- In a large mixing bowl combine cabbage, shredded carrots, bacon and blue cheese crumbles.
- In a separate bowl combine the rest of the ingredients using a whisk.
- Bring the sauce together with the cabbage mixture until fully incorporated.
- Best when served after chilled 4-8 hours.
- Yields about 4–6 servings

MARINATED KALE

Vegetarian, Vegan, Gluten-Free

Kale is an unruly superfood. It is truly packed with nutrients, including about 11 days worth of vitamin K per serving and nearly 100% of the recommended daily dose of Vitamin A. But to get through the occasionally tough texture, you have to massage it (seriously) or cook it. A third route is this tasty marinade, which gets a fresh bite from the ginger and lemon juice.

INGREDIENTS

4 cups packed kale

3 Tbsp olive oil

1/2 Tbsp sesame oil

1 Tbsp liquid aminos

1 Tbsp rice wine vinegar

1 Tbsp lemon juice

4 tsp fresh ginger

1/8 tsp white pepper

1/8 tsp salt

DIRECTIONS:

- De-stem and tear kale into 2-inch pieces.
- Wash kale and drain.
- Combine all other ingredients in blender and blend until thoroughly combined.
- Toss marinade with the kale in a large container and cover.
- Yield: about 4 cups packed

Marinated Kale

PARSNIPS

Vegetarian, Vegan, Gluten-Free

You can see how tasty a recipe is with the Garlic Index. With five cloves for about six parsnips, this recipe has an exceptionally favorable 5/6 ratio. Caveat: the Index does not apply to beverages or desserts.

INGREDIENTS

1 pound fresh parsnips (about 6)

1 Tbsp olive oil

5 whole garlic cloves

1/2 tsp salt

1/4 tsp white pepper

1 sprig rosemary

DIRECTIONS:

- Preheat oven to 350°F.
- Peel and wash parsnips.
- Cut into 2 to 3-inch strips at 1/2 to 1/4-inch thickness.
- Pull rosemary off sprig and roughly chop.
- Toss parsnips with olive oil, salt, pepper, rosemary and garlic cloves.
- Place on a buttered baking sheet and roast in oven for about 30 minutes, stirring halfway through.
- Garlic should be roasted slightly golden brown.
- Yield: about 7 cups

SALMON SALAD

Gluten-Free

Don't try this recipe if you like tuna salad—it's so tasty you'll never want to go back to the old canned tuna days again. Brining the fish first makes it extremely moist and flavorful, so you shouldn't skip that step.

INGREDIENTS

1 pound salmon filet

6 Tbsp mayo

1 tsp brown mustard

1 tsp black pepper

1/2 cup diced red onion

1/2 cup diced celery

2 Tbsp chopped tarragon

Fish Brine:

2 cups water

2 Tbsp salt

3 tsp sugar

1 ½ tsp lemon juice

DIRECTIONS:

Fish Brine:

- Add all ingredients to stock pot.
- Cook over high heat to dissolve salt and sugar (no need to boil).
- Remove from heat and cool.

Salmon:

- Preheat oven to 375°F.
- Dice salmon into 3/4-inch cubes.
- Brine salmon for 1 hour.
- Once salmon has brined, place on a baking sheet.
- Roast in 375°F oven for 15 minutes.
- Remove from oven and cool in refrigerator.

Salad:

- Once salmon is cooled, add to a medium mixing bowl.
- Add mayo, mustard, pepper, onion, celery and tarragon and gently fold until fully incorporated.
- Yield: about 6 cups

CUBAN BLACK BEANS

Vegetarian, Vegan, Gluten-Free

Trade relations are now loosening between the U.S. and Cuba, but for a long time, food was one of the few bridges that connected the two countries. These healthy and flavorful beans are cooked slowly and without meat, then topped with fresh pineapple and cilantro.

INGREDIENTS

4 cups cooked black beans

1/2 Tbsp canola oil

1/2 cup diced onions (about 1/2 medium onion)

1/2 Tbsp fresh garlic puree (about 2 cloves)

1 Tbsp cumin

1/2 cup water

1 Tbsp cider vinegar

2-ounce can diced green chiles

Topping:

1/2 cup pineapple, diced into 1/4-inch pieces

2 Tbsp chopped cilantro

DIRECTIONS:

- Preheat oven to 375°F.
- Sauté canola oil, onions, garlic, and cumin over medium heat in a large pan.
- Remove from heat and add beans, chiles, vinegar and water and stir together thoroughly.
- Transfer to an 8x8 pan and back in 375°F oven for one hour.
- Before serving, top with diced pineapple and cilantro.
- Yields 6 servings

MARINARA SAUCE

Vegetarian, Vegan, Gluten-Free, Fast and Easy

Doesn't marinara sauce have meat in it? No, you're thinking of Bolognese. You can serve this raw sauce on pasta for an ultra-light summer supper or with swirls of zucchini for a totally raw meal.

INGREDIENTS

2.5 cups fresh whole tomatoes (stem removed)

3/4 cups sundried tomatoes

1/4 cup olive oil

2 tablespoons chopped parsley

1 teaspoon salt

1 teaspoon agave

1/4 teaspoon granulated garlic

1/4 teaspoon dry basil

1/4 teaspoon oregano

1/4 teaspoon marjoram

pinch white pepper

pinch cayenne pepper

DIRECTIONS:

- Place all ingredients in food processor or blender and blend until semi smooth.
- Before serving, blend at high speed for 3 minutes. This warms it to about 115 degrees and improves the texture.
- Yield: about 3 cups

Bonus Tip:

Although you may be tempted to spill a lot of cayenne pepper into the sauce when trying to add just a little, avoid this temptation! It renders the sauce quite spicy!

QUINOA PILAF

Vegetarian, Vegan, Gluten-Free With peas, carrot, and mint, this light pilaf is perfect for spring-time. Serve it alongside braised lamb for an Easter dinner.

INGREDIENTS

1 cup quinoa

2 cups vegetable stock

1/4 tsp cayenne

1/2 cup peas

1/2 cup diced carrot

10 chiffonade mint or basil leaves

DIRECTIONS:

- Add vegetable stock, cayenne, and water to stock pot, cover and bring to a boil.
- Add quinoa and mix until fully incorporated.
- Put cover back on and cook for 20 minutes.
- Steam carrots until they are soft. Rinse with cold water to cool.
- Once pilaf is finished cooking mix in carrots, peas and mint or basil.
- Yield: 3 cups

Quinoa Pilaf

THE PEOPLE BEHIND THE FOOD
BAY PRODUCE

During the peak of the Lime Shortage of 2014, limes were nearly four times as expensive as average. Margaritas, pico de gallo, and similar basic necessities cost so much that Mexican drug cartels were getting in on the action. But Bay Produce, Duluth Grill's main tomato supplier, is one of the good guys. Work services director Debra Gergen says that when shortages come, the company keeps its prices the same.

"We would never raise our prices because somebody's unfortunate situation in another state," Debra says. "We aren't going to take advantage of a tomato crisis or freezing in Florida, drought, etc, because it has been the community that has supported us."

Bay Produce is based in Superior, Wisconsin, which is right across the bridge from the Duluth Grill. It is a part of the Challenge Center, a charity that is unfortunately all too familiar with people who take advantage of others. That's because beyond just producing tomatoes, the goal of the Challenge Center is giving real work experience to those who could use a bit of a hand.

"We aren't going to take advantage of a tomato crisis or freezing in Florida, drought, etc, because it has been the community that has supported us."

"Our job at the Challenge Center is to support individuals with developmental disabilities in their life and to make them successful," Debra says. "Other places have come up to look at Bay Produce to see if it is something they can put together and do and not many have chosen to follow through with it."

The first half acre greenhouse was built in 1986 for training and beefsteak tomatoes. By 1996, demand had increased to the point where the center built an additional 1-acre greenhouse. By 2008, the center had added bell peppers and cherry tomatoes and was at full production in both facilities. While many tomatoes from other producers are picked green and force-ripened, Bay Produce ripens its tomatoes on the vine for superior flavor.

"Our tomatoes are ripened the way a tomato should ripen from the inside to the outside," Debra says. "That is going to be the big difference in our quality is it tastes the way a tomato should taste."

Bay Produces uses a semi-hydroponic model (which isn't as easy as it looks—see page 34 for the Duluth Grill's own struggles with hydroponics). Instead of growing the vegetables in the dirt, they grow them in a combination of coconut fibers and nutrient-rich fertilized water. This, combined with the greenhouses, keeps away insects and allows for a more controlled growing environment. Bay Produce uses bumble bees for pollination and consistently rotates old and new plants.

The tomatoes are sold in Superior, Duluth, Two Harbors, Grand Rapids, and Cloquet. Bay Produce doesn't break even financially, but by providing good local food and employment for 25 developmentally disabled individuals, it builds up the community.

"People who work at Bay Produce are very proud of what they do," Debra says. "We need them to make it happen." DG

THE PEOPLE BEHIND THE FOOD
AU BON CANARD

Do you remember the movie *The Mighty Ducks*? Coach Bombay (Emilio Estevez) tells the team that ducks never get attacked, because if you mess with one duck, you mess with them all. Aside from the fact that that's not technically true, it's a good motto for a hockey team. And it's a good motto for Au Bon Canard as well. This 60-acre Caledonia farm, whose name means "Good Duck" in French, features plenty of duck teamwork.

The ducks stick together when they're still growing their feathers in the heated barn. They stick together when they're playing outside and taking mud baths. And they stick together until the end, when they're humanely killed and sold off to local restaurants. Proprietors Liz and Christian Gasset raise around 2,000 ducks per year and conditions are excellent.

"I know I am taking care of the ducks," Christian says. "And they have a really good life up until we use them, you know."

Christian was born in France, where duck is part of the culture.

"When I grew up in the south of France if you have some land you are going to raise 10 or 15 ducks for the family consumption," Christian says.

Christian met his wife Liz in Africa when she was serving in the Peace Corps. After falling in love they moved to Minnesota and decided to raise ducks. The rolling hills of the region where the farm is located are similar to those in the Pyrenees, where Christian was raised.

"You know I love it so much that I wanted to do this and I wanted to live on a farm," Christian says. "So I went back to school. You know when you want to do something for a living you have to learn everything about it so I went back to school and learned all about it before I started."

Christian's philosophy is intensely small scale and personalized. Each duck gets white glove treatment. It's sort of like if Christian were a concierge, and the farm were a Hilton, except for in this Hilton, you get eaten after your stay. So perhaps the analogy breaks down. But by feeding the ducks a high-quality diet, giving them individual attention and letting them roam in the fresh air, Christian ends up with stress-free, high quality meat.

And like the Mighty Ducks, Christian wants local growers and local restaurants to stick together. He wants to know whom he's selling to and he wants the restaurateurs to know him, so he keeps sales nearby.

"I do some shipping but speedy delivery so they just go in the state of Minnesota," Christian says. "I'm not going further than that." DG

Big Hearty Entrees

BA-BEETZA

Vegetarian, Gluten-Free

The official song is sung to the tune of *La Bamba* by Richie Valens. Here's the first verse:

Para hacer Ba-Beetza, para hacer Ba-Beetza se necesita una corteza de pizza.
Una corteza de pizza pa' mi, pa' ti, ay Ba-Beetza Ba-Beetza. Ay,
Ba-Beetza Ba-Beetza te comeré, te comeré, te comeré.

INGREDIENTS

1 gluten free pizza crust (you can also make this on pita, naan, or foccacia bread.)

2 Tbsp fresh tarragon

2 Tbsp fresh basil

1/4 cup olive oil

1/2 cup diced roasted beets (3/8-inch)

1/4 cup blue cheese crumbles

1/4 skinned and sliced fresh apple (1/8-inch)

1 Tbsp orange juice

1 egg white

2 cups pecans

1 Tbsp brown sugar

1 tsp salt

1/2 tsp ground chipotle pepper

3 Tbsp diced red onion (1/8-inch)

1/2 cup shredded cheddar cheese

Cooking spray

DIRECTIONS:

- Place the olive oil in a small bowl with the tarragon and basil, allow to sit for 2 hrs.
- Preheat oven to 225°F, in a mixing bowl combine the orange juice and egg white, add pecans.
- In a separate bowl combine brown sugar, salt and chipotle pepper. Add to pecan mixture, toss well.
- Spray a sheet pan with cooking spray and spread spiced pecan mixture out evenly, bake for 45 min.
- Preheat oven to 350°F, wrap the beet airtight in aluminum foil and bake for 80-90 minutes or until tender.
- Spread the tarragon basil oil on top of the GF pizza crust.
- First layer the sliced apple and diced roasted beets.
- Second layer blue cheese and shredded cheese.
- Third layer add chipotle pecans and onions.
- Bake on a sheet pan for 10-15 minutes at 350°F.
- Yields about 8 pieces

Year of the Beet

Every year the Duluth Community Garden Program celebrates a certain vegetable. 2012 was the Year of the Beet and it inspired the creation of this gluten-free, veggie-forward pizza.

THAI PIZZA

Vegetarian, Gluten-Free, Fast and Easy

This recipe is more of a guideline–ingredient amounts and ingredients themselves can be varied depending on personal taste. Consider yourself released to get in touch with your inner Escoffier.

INGREDIENTS

Ready-made gluten free pizza crust, or try this on pita, naan, or foccacia bread

½ cup peanut sauce

½ cup thinly sliced mushrooms

½ cup sliced roasted red peppers

½ cup feta cheese

fresh basil and cilantro to finish

DIRECTIONS:

- Place crust on baking pan.
- Spread peanut sauce on crust and top with mushrooms, red peppers and feta cheese, along with any other ingredients you'd like to add.
- Bake according to crust directions. Finish with a chiffonade of basil and cilantro.
- Yields: 1 pizza

ROLLED FLANK STEAK

Gluten-Free

Goat cheese, red peppers, and basil make a really nice pasta topping. But who needs pasta when you can just serve up the same flavors on delicious steak instead?

INGREDIENTS

1 flank steak

1 cup (8 ounces) goat cheese

2 roasted red peppers

8 large leaves of fresh basil

Salt and pepper

Balsamic reduction in a squeeze bottle

DIRECTIONS:

- Preheat oven to 450°F.
- Pound flank steak out until 1/4-inch thick.
- Season both sides with salt and pepper.
- Lay fresh basil down the middle of the flank steak from end to end.
- Cut roasted red peppers in half and lay out flat on flank steak from end to end.
- Top roasted red pepper with goat cheese.
- Starting with the long side of the flank steak start tightly rolling until flank steak is completely rolled up.
- Tie flank steak with butcher's twine.
- Place on baking sheet and bake at 450°F for 10 minutes.
- Reduce heat to 300°F and bake until the internal temperature reaches 135°F (about 30 minutes)
- Let rest for a few minutes before cutting.
- Cut into 1-inch portions in the same direction as the roll.
- Finish each plate with a drizzle of balsamic reduction.
- Yield: about 10 slices

DUCK CONFIT

Gluten-Free

There are a lot of possible ways to cook duck—you could grill it, bake it, or barbecue it. Or you could braise it slowly in its own fat until it's meltingly soft. This is why the French lead the world in cooking. This isn't a true braise, but the garbanzo flour mixes with the fat to form a tasty crust.

INGREDIENTS

Braise:

3/4 cup garbanzo flour (or other gluten free flour)

1 1/2 tsp black pepper

1 1/2 tsp thyme

1 tsp salt

1 duck cut into parts (breasts, thighs, legs)

canola oil as needed

Bake:

1 pound of rendered duck fat (2 cups)

4 quartered garlic cloves

1/2 tsp black pepper

sprig of rosemary

Braise:

DIRECTIONS:

- Mix the flour together with all the spices.
- Pour 1-inch of canola oil into a large sauté pan and turn flame on medium high heat.
- While oil is heating, coat duck pieces with flour mixture
- Place duck pieces in hot oil skin side down.
- Cook each side until golden brown (1-2 minutes on each side)
- Set aside once pieces are braised.

Bake:

- Place duck pieces bone side up in a small baking dish (should fit snugly)
- Melt duck fat and pour evenly over braised duck
- Sprinkle garlic and pepper over braised duck and place rosemary sprig on top
- Cover tightly with aluminum foil (should be airtight)
- Place in oven at 275F for 3 hours
- Yield: 1 duck (2 breasts, 2 thighs, 2 legs)

BEEF & PORK CHILI

Gluten-Free

A touch of chocolate and a tangy hint of balsamic vinegar are the secret touches to this otherwise classic chili recipe. With its big yield of two gallons this is ideally sized for a potluck or a large family gathering.

INGREDIENTS

1 pound ground beef

1 pound shredded pork butt or ground pork

1/2 cup chili powder

4 Tbsp cumin

4 Tbsp oregano

2 tsp black pepper

1/2 tsp cayenne pepper

2 cups diced onion (about 1 large onion)

2 Tbsp minced garlic

1 cup diced celery (about 2 stalks)

2 cups diced bell peppers (about 2 peppers)

1 diced jalapeño pepper

2 Tbsp chicken base

2 cups water

2 cups or 1 15-ounce can cooked black beans

2 cups or 1 15-ounce can cooked garbanzo beans

2 cups or 15-ounce can cooked kidney beans

2 28-ounce cans stewed tomatoes

2 28-ounce cans crushed tomatoes

4 2-ounce cans diced green chiles

1/3 cup balsamic vinegar

1-ounce dark chocolate pieces

2 tsp sugar

DIRECTIONS:

- Brown ground beef and ground pork (if using shredded pork, add after beef is halfway cooked)
- Add all spices and cook for about 3 minutes.
- Add the rest of the ingredients and stir until fully incorporated.
- Cover and reduce heat to low.
- Simmer for about an hour.
- Yield: about 2 gallons

SWEDISH MEATBALLS

The joke in Minnesota is that everyone eats lutefisk. The truth in Minnesota is that everyone eats Swedish meatballs. Along with tater tot hot dish and Jello salad, it's one of the true potluck staples. Best served with mashed potatoes after a 4:30pm sunset and a youth hockey game. Note that this will feed a crowd—there are 3 pounds of meat in here after all!

INGREDIENTS

Cooking spray

Meatballs:

2 medium onions

2 1/2 Tbsp butter

1 cup 2 percent milk

2 cups Japanese bread crumbs

3 eggs

1 pound ground pork

2 pounds ground beef

2 tsp salt

1 1/2 tsp nutmeg

1 1/2 tsp ground cardamom

1 Tbsp black pepper

Sauce:

3 Tbsp butter

3 Tbsp flour

1 Tbsp beef base

6 Tbsp sour cream

1/4 tsp salt

2 cups water

DIRECTIONS:

Meatballs:

- Grate onions in food processor or using a cheese grater.
- Melt butter in large skillet and sauté onions until they soften and turn translucent.
- Remove from heat and let cool.
- In a medium bowl add milk and bread crumbs together.
- Let sit until all milk is absorbed by the bread crumbs.
- Add cooled onions to bread crumbs.
- Add salt, nutmeg, cardamom and pepper to bread crumbs and mix well.
- Add beef, pork and eggs to bread crumb mixture and mix until fully incorporated.
- Let rest for 10 minutes.
- Preheat oven to 400°F.
- Line two baking sheets with aluminum foil and spray with a nonstick spray.
- Form meatballs using a small cookie scoop or a rounded tablespoon so they are about 1 1/4-inch in diameter.
- Place meatballs onto baking sheets.

- Brown in oven until they are golden brown and reach an internal temperature of 160°F.

Sauce:
- Melt butter in a small saucepan and add flour to make a roux.
- In separate saucepan mix water, beef base and salt and bring to a boil.
- Add roux to water mixture and whisk to make gravy.
- Once gravy is thickened, turn off heat and add sour cream.
- Stir until fully incorporated.
- Once meatballs are cooked, pour gravy over meatballs in a serving dish.
- Yield: about 50 meatballs

LEMON CHICKEN

Gluten-Free

Chicken, capers, and cream. The Cs have it with this hearty dinner option, with a sauce that's rich and tangy at the same time.

INGREDIENTS

6 chicken breasts
1 Tbsp olive oil
2 Tbsp lemon juice
1 Tbsp chicken base
1/2 cup water
1/2 tsp salt
1/2 tsp white pepper
2 Tbsp butter
2 Tbsp corn starch
1 cup cream
1 Tbsp drained capers

DIRECTIONS:

- Preheat oven to 350°F.
- Add olive oil, lemon juice, chicken base, salt, white pepper and water to a blender.
- Blend until emulsified.
- In a sauce pan add emulsion and butter, bring to a simmer.
- Mix the corn starch and cream in a separate container to make a slurry.
- Whisk in slurry at a simmer.
- Add capers.
- Pour sauce over chicken breasts and bake for about 40 minutes or until the internal temperature of the chicken reaches 165°F.
- Yield: 6 chicken breasts

PAELLA

Gluten-Free

This is paella from an alternate timeline where Spain won the Spanish-American War so decisively that it conquered Minnesota too. There's wild instead of regular rice and whitefish instead of Pacific seafood, in addition to Mediterranean touches like roasted red peppers, capers, and olive oil.

INGREDIENTS

1 cup dry wild rice

2 cups water

1/2 cup olive oil

1 ½ cup sliced roasted red peppers

2 cups tomato filets (about 3 medium peeled tomatoes)

1/4 cup minced garlic (about 8 medium cloves)

1 ½ tsp thyme

1 ½ tsp smoked paprika

8 cups chicken stock

fish brine (recipe page 22)

2–3 pounds of fresh raw fish (Duluth Grill has used salmon and halibut but you can use most kinds of fish or even shellfish)

one cup of sweet peas (fresh or frozen)

chopped flat leaf parsley to finish

DIRECTIONS:

- Cut fish into 1-inch dice and place in brine in refrigerator for one hour.
- Place paella pan (or other large sauté pan) on stove top and set to medium heat.
- Add olive oil and allow oil to heat up.
- Add tomato fillets, roasted red peppers, minced garlic and sauté for 2 minutes.
- Add seasonings and cook for an additional minute.
- Reduce heat to medium.
- Add wild rice and mix until fully incorporated.
- Add 2 cups of chicken stock and simmer until rice is cooked adding more stock as needed. Stir often. While the rice is cooking, it will start to absorb the chicken stock. When it becomes dry, this is the time to add more stock. Continue adding stock until it's absorbed.
- When all the stock is nearly absorbed, add fish and peas. Continue cooking until fish is just opaque.
- Top with flat leaf parsley.
- Yield: 6–8 servings

Note:

If you cook this ahead of time, keep the paella warm and don't add the fish until the end. This prevents it from being overcooked

FLANK STEAK LEMON GRASS

Gluten-Free

Besides sweet, sour, salty, and bitter, there is a fifth taste. Called *umami*, it can broadly be translated as "savory richness" and in western culture encompasses grilled steak, ketchup, and Parmesan cheese, for example. But umami is found even more strongly in Asian flavors like fish sauce (*nam pla*) and oyster sauce. This flank steak recipe contains both.

INGREDIENTS

2 pounds beef flank steak
salt to season
ground black pepper to season

Marinade:

3 Tbsp gluten-free oyster sauce (use regular oyster sauce if you're not gluten intolerant)
1/3 cup sugar
1/2 tsp salt
1/2 tsp cayenne pepper
2 medium minced garlic cloves
1 stalk chopped lemongrass: pound out and cut into 1/8-inch slices
3 Tbsp fish sauce

Make it a Bowl

Top this with the curry sauce from page 13. We like to serve this as a bowl with wild rice, broccoli, red peppers, mushrooms and onions. You could also try quinoa, couscous, and different vegetables.

DIRECTIONS:

- In a blender, mix all marinade ingredients. Set aside.
- Cover a cutting board with plastic wrap.
- Place the flank steak on the lined cutting board and cover with another piece of plastic wrap.
- Pound the flank steak to 1/2-inch thick.
- Remove the plastic wrap and season the steak on both sides with salt and pepper.
- Cut the steak into 1/2-inch cubes.
- Place the meat into the marinade and allow to marinate covered in the refrigerator overnight.
- Stir fry to desired doneness.
- Yield: 5 cups cooked

BISON STUFFED PEPPERS

Gluten-Free

One of the best ways to serve these is in warm flour or corn tortillas with sour cream and extra stuffing mix. Where do you find bison? Check your local co-op or whole foods store or search online on bisoncentral.com for local or online vendors.

INGREDIENTS

2 Tbsp canola oil

1 cup diced onion

1½ tsp chopped garlic

2 Tbsp pork rub

1/2 lb shredded bison roast or ground bison

2 cups tomato filets

1 cup cooked wild rice

4 2-ounce cans diced green chiles

3/4 cup shredded cheddar

8 Anaheim peppers

DIRECTIONS

- Add 2 Tbsp canola oil in a sauté pan and lightly sauté onions and garlic over medium high heat.
- Add pork rub to onions and cook down.
- Add chiles and tomato filets, then add bison and let simmer for 15 minutes.
- Add wild rice and cheese and cook until cheese melts and rice is warm.
- Place a cast iron skillet over high heat.
- Cut the ends off of the Anaheim peppers and place the peppers in the skillet.
- Lightly char the outside of the peppers.
- Remove peppers from skillet and place stuffing into peppers.
- Yield: 8 stuffed Anaheim peppers

Pepper Patrol:

A caution about Anaheim peppers: the fresher they are, the spicier they will be! They do have a good kick to them, but you can always cut the peppers into smaller pieces and add more stuffing if you don't like so much heat. Use caution when blackening them on the stove.

DUCK BURGER

Gluten-Free

Duck is a relatively mild bird, but it's slightly gamier and slightly richer than chicken. Barbecue sauce and sugar provide sweetness, and heat from sriracha and black pepper combine with garlic, basil, and green onion to round out the spice.

INGREDIENTS:

1 pound duck breast (about 2 large breasts) or ground duck

4 chiffonade basil leaves

2 chopped green onion stocks

1 tsp minced garlic (about 2 cloves)

1 Tbsp barbecue sauce

1/2 Tbsp sugar

1/2 Tbsp sriracha

1 Tbsp corn starch

1/2 tsp black pepper

1/2 tsp salt

DIRECTIONS:

- Roughly chop duck and grind through a meat grinder, or dice it very finely.
- In a medium mixing bowl, mix all ingredients lightly.
- Form into 6 medium burgers (This won't come together quite as well as standard beef burgers, so feel free to just plop it in a pan or griddle in scoops).
- Place on baking sheet and bake for 30-35 minutes at 350°F.
- Turn over and grill both sides to an internal temperature of 165°F.
- Yield: 4 cups

Tip:

How do you turn a duck patty into a fully loaded duck burger? A toasted bun spread with paté, carrot daikon slaw, cilantro, pickled jalapenos, and sriracha aioli should do the trick.

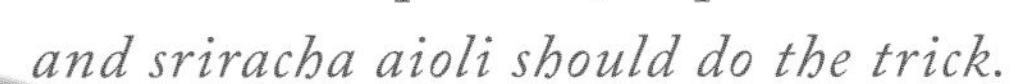

COUNTRY PATÉ

Gluten-free

Serve this soft, rich pate on bread or crackers, or on a platter with fruit and cheese for a gluten-free appetizer.

INGREDIENTS:

1/4 finely chopped medium yellow onion

1/2 pound chicken livers

2 finely chopped garlic cloves

1/2 pound ground pork sausage

1/2 tsp Chinese 5 spice powder

2 tsp fish sauce

1 tsp sugar

1 tsp salt

DIRECTIONS:

- Preheat oven to 275F.
- Add onion, garlic, sausage, fish sauce, Chinese 5 Spice, sugar and salt to a mixing bowl and mix well.
- Puree liver in a food processor.
- Add pureed livers to mixing bowl and mix until fully incorporated.
- Pack into a loaf pan.
- Place loaf pan into a water bath (water should be even with the paté dish)
- Bake at 275°F until internal temperature reaches 165°F (about one hour)
- Remove from water bath to cool.
- Yield: one loaf pan

PORK ON A STICK

Gluten-Free

In Minnesota's early history, the state fair was a rare and precious opportunity for farm kids to socialize with someone besides their siblings and the livestock. Now, it's mostly an opportunity to eat things on sticks. This is a fun party snack that lets the fair come to you.

INGREDIENTS

1 pork loin

Brine:

1/4 cup honey

1/4 cup cider vinegar

1/4 cup salt

1 cup water

1/8 tsp ground clove

1/8 tsp cinnamon

1/4 tsp granulated garlic

1 bay leaf

1/8 tsp ground ginger

3 cups ice cold water

DIRECTIONS:

- Slice pork loin into medallions (about 3-ounce pieces), set aside.
- In a stock pot, combine all ingredients (minus 3 cups ice cold water).
- Heat until salt has dissolved.
- Remove brine from heat and add 3 cups ice cold water.
- Place pork medallions in a large container and pour brine over pork.
- Cover and brine overnight in refrigerator.
- Once pork has brined overnight, remove pork from brine and let rest on a baking sheet for 30 minutes.
- Place 6-inch skewers into each medallion so they look like lollipops.
- Grill or bake until internal temperature reaches 160°F.
- Yield: 12 3-ounce medallions

BARBECUED EGGPLANT

Vegetarian, Gluten-Free

Vegetarians do themselves a disservice when they say something's "just as good as" a similar meat dish. What about "better than"? Come on, vegetarians; show some fighting spirit! Eggplant is better than meat for barbecue because it has the same robust texture and smoky char, but absorbs seasonings better and has a noticeable creaminess of its own.

INGREDIENTS

4 medium eggplants

2 Tbsp pork rub

6 Tbsp barbecue sauce

1 Tbsp sesame oil

DIRECTIONS:

- Grill whole eggplants over high heat for 20 minutes, turning every few minutes until eggplants are charred on the outside and • cooked throughout.
- Place eggplant in a large container and cover
- Place the container in the refrigerator
- Once eggplant is cooled, pull the skin off
- Pull the insides of the eggplant apart. This will resemble pulled pork.
- Place eggplant in a medium mixing bowl and add dry rub. Mix until eggplant is seasoned well.
- Line a 9x13 pan or a cookie sheet with parchment paper and spread out eggplant so it is in a single layer.
- Bake in oven at 250°F for 1½ hours.
- Increase heat to 350°F and bake an additional 15 minutes.
- Remove eggplant and place into a mixing bowl.
- Add barbecue sauce and sesame oil and toss until eggplant is well coated.
- Yield: 4 cups

RAISING A FAMILY AT THE GRILL

While the core of this book is sweetness, light, and (arguably) hilarious jokes, there are some dark spots to running a business as all consuming as a family restaurant. The Duluth Grill is family-friendly enough to keep away the worst of the blights—it doesn't serve alcohol or stay open past 9 pm, so the staff has mostly avoided the hard-partying culture that sometimes ruins lives with addiction or DWIs. There's a strong sense of camaraderie, and the managers set the pace by working hard and paying well. But that dedication to the business can be a double-edged sword when it comes to raising a family.

Louis Hanson is the back of the house manager and Tom and Jaima's son. He got into the restaurant business in high school, where it was a good way to have fun, learn work habits, and earn some money at the same time. When he married his wife, Ashley, she soon learned that marrying into a restaurant family means marrying into a restaurant.

"We were in Vegas and his parents were like 'you have to start working at the restaurant," Ashley says. "I was scared'.

She found her calling as a server, where her easy smile and charm allowed her to connect quickly with customers (it didn't hurt when it came to tips either). But when their first son Peyton was born, time together became scarce. Ashley says Louis switched from managing to serving to try to get more time together.

"I didn't like him managing all the time because I'd never see him, he'd be out until 2 in the morning." Ashley says.

Back: Whitney, Willow & Dan LeFebvre; Caden, Jeff, Corbin & Julie Petcoff
Seated: Parker (back), Peyton (front), Ashley & Louis Hanson

"There are also days where you have that baseball game and it's so busy—there's catering, a line out the door, it just keeps mounting and mounting. When the fires are burning you put them out. That's the commitment part, above and beyond everything else."

But it soon became clear that juggling two server schedules wasn't substantially easier.

"I served at night and he did mornings," Ashley says. "We still didn't see each other. He went back to managing."

Louis says that he wants his kids to get the experience of working in a restaurant. He says that when you're younger, it offers a good lifestyle while teaching hard work. That said, he feels like it's a tough fit for a family.

"It's a bad idea," he says. "I'm here and not there."

General manager Jeff Petcoff, who also has young children, has faced different challenges. He's been working at the Grill since he was 17 and says when he started dating his wife Julie, the Duluth Grill helped him seal the deal.

"The first time I made dinner for her was a Duluth Grill dish," Jeff says. "Tom helped me work through the recipe and I got all the ingredients from here. It really impressed her--I have Tom to thank for that."

But it's not all roses and spicy Thai pasta with peanut sauce. Jeff says Julie has had to deal with irregular and often long hours.

"My wife's not in this business," Jeff says. "There's a learning curve to it for sure."

The Petcoffs are also raising two children. Corbin is almost 5 and Caden is almost 10, and Jeff says he and Julie try to plan their schedules so they can watch the kids' games.

"[You] set yourself up so those things can happen," Jeff says. "Those are the important things you can't take back as a dad."

The management team works to try to cover each other's backs on those days. On the other hand, Jeff says there are times all hands have to be on deck.

"There's also days where you have that baseball game and it's like 'it's so busy, there's catering, a line out the door, it just keeps mounting and mounting'," Jeff says. "When the fires are burning you put them out. That's the commitment part, above and beyond everything else."

Ultimately, Jeff says, it's a question of balance. He sometimes expects Julie to just automatically set everything up with the kids, and he needs to pitch in more. On the other hand, sometimes Julie and the kids just want him home.

"I think she'll always want me to be home more and the kids want me to be home more than I am," Jeff says.

"If we can finally teach him to get the hell out of here when he needs to get out of here!" Don Doane pipes in.

Server Whitney LeFebvre knows what it's like to have a spouse working long hours. She met her husband Dan eight years ago when he came to work as a cook at the Grill. Now that he's the kitchen manager, he often works from 7 to 7 or even longer. At the same time, she's taking care of Willow, who was just over two months old when this book was being written. Dan and Whitney have been married six years and both say they work at having time together, whether it's planning the same days off or being together in the evenings.

"It's easy to get upset and to be frustrated with how much he works," Whitney says. "I try to be understanding and just be supportive. In the evenings I make sure I'm home when he gets home so we can have a little time every day."

All three couples mentioned here are doing this for the sake of a dream. But there's no denying that the restaurant business takes its toll. The family feeling of having a close staff that fights through thick and thin is exhilarating. At the same time, there are sacrifices.

"I wouldn't want this life for anybody unless you want it," Louis says. DG

Desserts

FLORENTINES

Vegetarian

We have to credit Dexter Larson for teaching us his skills on this cookie. You might be surprised to see corn syrup in this book. But the stuff is ok in moderation—after all, baking isn't a religion and corn syrup isn't evil personified. In fact, in a dessert like these cookies, it helps them get flat and crisp. (The main problem with corn syrup nowadays is that it's often found in dishes that aren't desserts at all, and if you eat sugar all day it's going to catch up with you!)

INGREDIENTS

- 7 Tbsp softened butter
- 7 Tbsp heavy cream
- 1 1/2 Tbsp corn syrup
- 1 cup plus 3 Tbsp sugar
- 1/4 cup flour
- 4 3/4 cup (about 1lb) sliced, raw almonds

DIRECTIONS

- Add butter, heavy cream, sugar, and corn syrup into a saute pan. Turn on medium high heat and bring to boil. Stir and remove from heat.
- Toss almonds and flour to thoroughly coat the almonds with flour.
- Combine warm liquid and almonds and mix thoroughly.
- Cover and chill for at least one hour. That is to say, chill the mixture. You can chill too if you'd like.
- Spoon 1-inch balls onto a lined baking sheet or silicon mat and flatten.
- Bake at 375°F for 5-10 minutes (These should triple in diameter and be quite thin).
- *Optional finish:* after cookies are done, dip in a melting chocolate and allow to set and cool.
- Yields about 16 florentines.

SUGAR COOKIES

Vegetarian, Vegan, Fast and Easy

The only problem with sugar cookies is that there are never quite enough of them. Coconut oil has similar properties to lard or Crisco but lends a subtle tropical flavor. Can you imagine these with some pineapple ice cream?

INGREDIENTS

1.5 cups powdered sugar
1 cup coconut oil (not melted)
1/4 cup vanilla coconut milk ×2
1 tsp vanilla
1/8 tsp salt
2.5 cups all-purpose flour
2 Tbsp cornstarch
1 tsp baking soda
1 tsp cream of tartar

DIRECTIONS

- Preheat oven to 350°F. on convection.
- Mix together powdered sugar, coconut oil, coconut milk, and vanilla until smooth.
- Add remaining ingredients and mix until fully incorporated (texture should be similar to pie crust dough).
- Roll out dough to 1/4-inch thick and use a cookie cutter or 1 cup measuring cup to cut out cookies. - Shot glass.
- Pick up the scraps, form into a ball, roll out and cut more cookies.
- Place the cookies on a lined baking sheet and bake for 10–15 minutes.
- Let cool on a cooling rack and enjoy!
- Yield: about 3 dozen cookies

Tip:

If the dough is difficult to handle, place it in the fridge or freezer for a few minutes to let it firm up

VELVET PUMPKIN CAKE

Vegetarian

There is nothing like a classic fall dessert. Top this with fresh whipped cream, cinnamon, and nutmeg.

INGREDIENTS:

1 box organic white cake mix

2 sticks softened butter

4 eggs

1 tsp vanilla

1 tsp cinnamon

1 tsp nutmeg

1 cup powdered sugar

15-ounce can pumpkin

8-ounce package of cream cheese

DIRECTIONS:

- Preheat oven to 350°F.
- Grease one 9x13 pan.
- In a medium bowl, combine 1 egg, 1 stick of butter, and cake mix.
- Mix well and pat cake mix into bottom of greased pan, this will be your crust.
- In a medium bowl, cream together 1 stick of butter, cream cheese, powdered sugar, 3 eggs and vanilla.
- Add pumpkin, cinnamon and nutmeg, mix well.
- Pour batter over cake mix crust.
- Bake for 45 minutes, check, if cake springs back when touched lightly in the center it is done. If not, bake it another 10 minutes and check again.
- Cool for 1 hour or until completely cooled.
- Yields: 1 cake

PUMPKIN BARS

Vegetarian, Fast and Easy

Pumpkin bars are a place for pumpkins 21 and older to relax with their friends and socialize with other pumpkins.

INGREDIENTS:

Pumpkin Bars

2 eggs

1 cup sugar

1/2 cup canola oil

1/2 15-ounce can pumpkin

1 cup all-purpose flour

1 tsp baking powder

1/2 tsp baking soda

1 tsp ground cinnamon

1/2 tsp salt

Frosting

1/2 cup soft butter

3 cups powdered sugar

1 Tbsp milk

3/4 tsp nutmeg

DIRECTIONS:

- Preheat oven to 350ºF.
- In a medium mixing bowl, mix egg, sugar, oil and pumpkin puree with mixer until light and fluffy.
- In another bowl, sift flour, baking soda, baking powder, cinnamon and salt. Stir the dry mix into pumpkin mixture until it is combined.
- Spread batter evenly in an ungreased 13x9 cake pan. Bake for 25-30 minutes or until a pick inserted in the middle comes out clean. Allow to cool completely before frosting.
- For frosting: place the butter and one cup of the powdered sugar into a mixing bowl. Add the milk and nutmeg, and mix until incorporated.
- While mixing, add the rest of the powdered sugar one cup at a time, and continue mixing until the frosting has a smooth consistency.
- Spread evenly over top of bars.
- Yield: one 13x9 pan

WHIPPED CREAM

Vegetarian, Gluten-Free, Fast and Easy

Ditch the Reddi-Whip, because homemade whipped cream is so easy an eleven year old can make it. But according to Duluth fifth grader Jessica Jones, you should make sure not to mix too long because it will start to turn to butter.

INGREDIENTS

2 cups heavy cream
(or heavy whipping cream)

1 tsp vanilla

1/3 cup powdered sugar

1/4 tsp cream of tartar

For chocolate: 1 tbsp cocoa powder

For mint: 5 Starlight mints crushed into a fine powder

DIRECTIONS

- In medium bowl, mix all ingredients on low speed until start to thicken.
- Once thickened, increase speed to high until stiff peaks form.
- Refrigerate leftovers.
- Yields: about two quarts

"Once my mom whipped cream so long water came out of it," Jessica said. "Actually, that was you," her older sister Annaliese piped in. "It wasn't mom." "It was?" Jessica said. "Oh."

CANNOLI SHELLS

Vegetarian

If you've ever run into the Cannoli Patrol (or heard their sirens as they drove past in a parking lot) you know getting between them and their cannoli is serious business. The Duluth Grill's version has the flavors of a zabaglione with cinnamon, coffee, and marsala wine.

INGREDIENTS

2 cups all-purpose flour

1 beaten egg

1/4 tsp cinnamon

2 Tbsp sugar

1 Tbsp olive oil

1/2 lemon zest

1 ½ tsp instant coffee

1/2 cup Marsala wine

1 quart canola oil for deep frying

roughly 8–10 cups of filling (see below)

DIRECTIONS

- Sift flour into a large mixing bowl. Add half the beaten egg, cinnamon, sugar, olive oil, lemon zest and instant coffee.
- Add Marsala wine, mixing by hand until ingredients come together to form a dough. Knead until firm and elastic.
- Chill several hours or overnight.
- Cut the dough into fourths and roll through a pasta machine until 1/8-inch thick. Cut out 4-inch circles. Sprinkle each disc with cinnamon and sugar.
- In a medium pot with a heavy bottom, heat 1 quart of canola oil to 360°F.
- Wrap a disk around a cannoli mold (or a 1-inch dowel) and brush seam with some of the beaten egg to seal. Deep fry until crispy, about 2 to 3 minutes. Repeat with remaining disks.
- How do you fill cannoli? For this size recipe, the Duluth Grill would use a blend of 32 ounces of ricotta cheese, one cup of powdered sugar, and 2 cups of heavy cream (whip separately and then fold into the other ingredients)—this will make a bit extra, but that's the Italian grandmother's way! You can fill them with pudding, mousse, whipped cream, custard, or even ice cream. Pipe it in with a pastry bag for best results.
- Makes about 24 cannoli shells

LAYERED CARROT CAKE

Vegetarian

Carrot cake is nice because it reduces things to the basics: if you find a whole carrot in there, you know someone did a bad job grating. This recipe almost did the recipe testers in. It took four tries to get it right, and wow, did they ever get it right. When you eat it, pause for a moment to reflect on those brave cooks who went before you.

INGREDIENTS

Cream Cheese Frosting

1 pound cream cheese (two 8-ounce packages) at room temperature

5 cups powdered sugar

1/2 pound butter (two sticks) at room temperature

2 tsp vanilla

Cake

2 1/2 cups all-purpose flour

2 tsp baking soda

1 tsp salt

1 tsp cinnamon

1/2 cup raisins

2 cups sugar

1 cup vegetable oil

2 tsp vanilla

2 eggs

2 cups diced or shredded carrots

8-ounce can crushed pineapple with juices

DIRECTIONS

- Grease and flour two 9-inch round cake pans.
- Preheat oven to 350°F.
- In a medium mixing bowl, sift together flour, baking soda, salt and cinnamon; add raisins and mix well.
- Shred carrots or pulse in a food processor several times, carrot pieces should be small like a pea.
- In a large mixing bowl, combine sugar, oil, vanilla and eggs; mix by hand with a wooden spoon until blended.
- Add the flour mixture and continue to mix by hand.
- Stir in carrots and pineapple with juices until mixed evenly.
- Pour and spread batter into greased and floured pans.
- Bake for 45–55 minutes depending on oven, check at 30 minutes but not before; using a toothpick, check for doneness, if it comes out clean, the cake is done.
- While the cake is baking, make the cream cheese frosting. In a mixer, combine all ingredients, mix well. There should be no lumps (sifting the sugar first will help with this).
- Remove cakes from oven and let sit in pans for 10 minutes. Then cut around the sides of the cake and place a plate or cooling rack on top of the pan, flip upside down and gently tap the bottom of the pan if cake does not come out of the pan right away.
- Cool in the refrigerator.
- When cake is cool, frost with cream cheese frosting. Using a large decorator bag with a large tip, frost the top (what was once the bottom) of one of the cake layers, refrigerate to stiffen up icing, once it has set up, put second layer on top of the first. Now frost the top and sides of the cake using a knife or spatula. If you feel creative and have the equipment, with orange and green frosting, pipe little carrots on top of the cake and a decorative edging around the bottom.
- Yield: one 9-inch cake with two layers

RED VELVET CUP CAKES

Vegetarian, Fast and Easy

The red velvet cake has a long and storied history… as a marketing gimmick. In the 1940s, American hero John A. Adams tricked out regular velvet cake with his FDA-approved red dye. The cakes spread everywhere, and food coloring sales spiked. The funny thing is that these cupcakes taste just as good without it.

Note:

These are especially good if you serve them with the cream cheese frosting from the carrot cake recipe on page 129.

INGREDIENTS

2 ½ cups all-purpose flour

1 ½ cups sugar

1 tsp baking soda

1 tsp salt

1 tsp cocoa powder

1 ½ cups vegetable oil

1 cup buttermilk at room temp

2 large eggs

1 tsp distilled white vinegar

1 tsp vanilla extract

2 Tbsp red food coloring

DIRECTIONS

- Preheat oven to 350°F.
- In a medium mixing bowl sift together flour, sugar, baking soda, salt, and cocoa powder.
- In a large bowl, beat together the oil, buttermilk, eggs, vinegar, vanilla, and food coloring.
- Add dry mix to the wet mix and mix until smooth and incorporated.
- Line muffin tins with liners. Fill each liner 2/3 full.
- Bake for 20-22 minute or until pick inserted comes out clean, allow to cool.
- Yield: approximately 24 cupcakes

Note:

For a natural form of red food coloring, substitute 1/4 cup of beet juice and double cocoa powder.

AVOCADO CHOCOLATE SORBET

Vegetarian, Vegan, Gluten-Free

Avocado is naturally creamy, so it's the perfect base for a vegan sorbet. This is technically a sorbet but tastes and feels more like an ice cream.

INGREDIENTS

Simple Syrup

1/2 cup water

1 cup sugar

1/8 tsp cream of tartar

1½ avocados

13.5-ounce can Thai coconut milk

1/2 tsp salt

1/4 cup cocoa powder

DIRECTIONS

- Mix water, sugar, and cream of tartar in a saucepan and bring to a simmer until sugar dissolves.
- Puree peeled avocados, coconut milk, salt, and cocoa powder.
- Pour mixture though a mesh strainer.
- Whisk in the simple syrup while still hot until mixture is smooth.
- Let cool at least 4 hours.
- Pour into ice cream machine and follow manufacturer's directions to freeze.
- Yield: about one quart

CINNAMON CHAI SORBET

Vegetarian, Vegan, Gluten-Free

"Chai" means "tea", so when you say "chai tea" you're saying "tea tea". It's sort of like "ATM machine" (the M stands for machine) or "PIN number" (the N stands for number). This is a good recipe recipe. Coconut milk makes it creamy, the squash gives it heft and body, and the spices in the syrup make it the perfect finale for an Indian-themed meal.

INGREDIENTS

1 1/2 cups roasted squash (3/4 lb roasted weight)

1 1/2 cups Chai tea (12-oz)

1 1/2 cups Thai coconut milk

enough olive oil to coat squash

2 tsp sea salt

Simple Syrup

3/4 cups sugar

1/3 cup water

3/4 tsp cinnamon

1/4 tsp nutmeg

1/8 tsp ginger

DIRECTIONS

- Combine all ingredients for simple syrup in a saucepan and bring to a boil, stirring constantly.
- Remove syrup from heat and set aside to cool.
- To roast squash, cut into 1-inch cubes and toss in olive oil and sea salt. Roast in a 375°F oven until well caramelized, cool. Weigh out needed amount.
- Puree Chai tea and squash in a food processor. Pass through a fine mesh strainer. Whisk in the coconut milk and simple syrup until combined. Pour into ice cream maker and freeze.
- Makes 7 cups

TARRAGON OLIVE OIL ICE CREAM

Vegetarian, Gluten-Free

This was mentioned in the last Duluth Grill Cookbook but it definitely bears repeating—tarragon, a popular French herb with a gentle licorice flavor, is also known as dragon's wort. Dragon's wort! It's also related to the delightfully alliterative Mexican Marigold Mint.

Note:

What should you do with the 12 leftover egg whites? Make meringues! Beat room temperature whites with an electric mixer in a spotlessly clean glass bowl until soft peaks form, then beat in a tablespoon of sugar at a time (1/4 cup per white) until the mixture doesn't slide out when you turn the bowl upside down. Spoon them out onto a baking sheet covered in parchment paper (dollops of about golf ball size or slightly larger). Bake the meringues at a lower temperature (250–325) for a longer time period (20–40 minutes) until you get the consistency you want. Don't do this on a humid day.

INGREDIENTS

2 2/3 cups 2% milk

1 cup sugar

2/3 tsp salt

12 egg yolks

2 cups heavy whipping cream

1 1/2 ounce fresh tarragon leaves (can be bought in containers of .75 of an ounce)

1 cups olive oil

Ice or snow for ice water bath

DIRECTIONS

- Combine milk, sugar and salt in medium sauce pot, bring mixture to a simmer and remove from heat.
- Using a ladle, temper egg yolks in a separate bowl from the hot ice cream base.
- Pour tempered eggs into the rest of the ice cream base while stirring constantly and return to medium heat.
- Remove hot ice cream base from heat once mixture reaches 185°F and pour through a strainer into a 13x9 pan for cooling, mix in cold heavy whipping cream and place in ice water bath (a large cookie sheet with sides packed with snow works well; you can put a lid on the 13x9 pan and cover with towels for insulation.) Let cool completely before moving on to the next step.
- Once ice cream base is cooled, pick the tarragon leaves off the stems, you will need a sauce pan with boiling water for blanching and a container with ice water for cooling (you may not want to use snow for this part).
- Blanch tarragon leaves in boiling water for 5-10 seconds, remove from water with a strainer and place in ice water bath. Tarragon should be bright green in color. Remove tarragon from ice bath, squeeze out all excess water and place in a blender.
- Add a cup of ice cream base to blender and blend well. Pour contents through a strainer.
- Add all ice cream base to blender and slowly increase speed. Pour olive oil into blender and mix until well incorporated, once again, pour contents through strainer.
- Pour mix back into the 13x9 pan and place in freezer. You can stir every 10 minutes for 30 minutes for creamier texture. Leave in freezer until it has the constancy of ice cream.
- Yield: about 6 cups

WHEN PIGS FLY

Gluten-Free, Fast and Easy

Assuming your scoops are 1/2 cup each and you're using 2 tablespoons of caramel sauce, this bad boy weighs in at about 900 calories. This is the kind of dessert you'll probably want to split with a friend.

INGREDIENTS

3 scoops vanilla ice cream

1/2 cup roasted pecans

2 strips of extra crispy bacon

Pinch of pink Hawaiian sea salt

Caramel sauce to top

DIRECTIONS

- Scoop vanilla ice cream in a circular motion from the outside of the container in to produce a tennis ball sized sphere.
- Cover one side with roasted pecans.
- Cover the other side with chopped, extra crispy bacon.
- Sprinkle pink Hawaiian sea salt over the top.
- Drizzle generously with caramel sauce and enjoy.
- Yield: 1 mega serving or 2 reasonable servings

AVOCADO MANGO SORBET

Vegetarian, Vegan, Gluten-Free

Put the lime in the coconut and shake it all up. Then, add the mangos and avocado. It's actually easier to use frozen mangoes for this dish since they're already peeled. And you're going to end up freezing them anyway (unless your cooking takes a dramatically wrong turn.)

INGREDIENTS

Sorbet base:

2 avocados

13.5-ounce can Thai coconut milk

10-ounces mangoes (fresh or frozen)

1/3 cup lime juice

1/2 tsp salt

1 cup simple syrup

1 cup vanilla coconut milk

Simple syrup:

1⅓ cup sugar

1⅓ cup water

1/8 tsp cream of tartar

DIRECTIONS

- For the simple syrup, mix water, sugar and cream of tartar in a saucepan, bring to a simmer and stir until sugar dissolves. Set aside to cool.
- For the sorbet, puree avocado, mangoes and Thai coconut milk in a food processor. Whisk in lime juice, simple syrup, and salt. Pass through a fine mesh strainer.
- Whisk in vanilla coconut milk. Pour into ice cream maker and freeze.
- Makes 7 cups

WHAT'S IN A NAME?

(Part Two)

From King Arthur and the Knights of the Round Table all the way through John Henry beating the steam coal shovel, every culture has its legends and heroes. In the first cookbook I wrote about how the Duluth Grill got its name. According to legend, an assistant manager back in the Prehansonic Era was on maternity leave watching *Days of Our Lives* and liked the sound of the fictional Port Charles Grille. So, they named the Duluth Grill accordingly.

But former owner Kay Biga tells a different story. She says that when buying the restaurant in the 80s, she also bought the rights to use the name Highway Host of Duluth, but only for five years.

"After five years we had to pay to use the name Highway Host," Kay says. "I thought, that's the most ridiculous thing I've ever heard, paying for the name when it's not a highway anymore."

Duluth Grill is a great name for the search engines since Duluth is right in the title, but in those dark, Wild West-like pre-Internet days, that wasn't a consideration. Instead, Kay says she was swimming at the Center For Personal Fitness and thinking about the simply named St. Paul Grill when she realized she could copy that name in Duluth.

"It popped into my head," Kay says. "Just like all my great ideas."

It's a pretty plausible story, especially since, if you really think about it, it's usually the owner and not the assistant manager on maternity leave who gets to name a restaurant. As much as Tom loves the idea of the soap opera, Kay says it just isn't what happened.

"I know it wasn't from a soap opera," Kay says. "Take it to the bank. Hook me up to a lie detector!" DG

"After five years we had to pay to use the name Highway Host," Kay says. "I thought, that's the most ridiculous thing I've ever heard, paying for the name when it's not a highway anymore."

REMOVING FRIES

Some things are easy to pull from the menu—like the raw kale salad nobody wanted to order. Other things are a little more difficult. The Duluth Grill started as a run-of-the-mill diner, and inherited a little group of customers that used to sit around for hours with a cup of coffee. When Tom pulled the tuna melt, you would have thought the Red Cross had started charging for doughnuts again.

Replacing store-bought ketchup with homemade and pulling fountain sodas were both difficult decisions as well. But it wasn't until the spring of 2014 when the Grill decided to mess with the most all-American snack of all.

You can still get hamburgers, you can still get apple pie, and you can still get Pepsi (in the bottle). But the French fries?

"We only have two deep fryers," Tom says. "We were trying to look at what could be eliminated from the fried food section. We said let's boil it down to what we sell the least of."

"Restaurants started offering French fries with food because they're super cheap, not because they're fabulous."

The onion rings were time consuming, but the handmade recipe meant they were also extremely popular. Smashed potatoes and sweet potato fries were favorites as well. But French fries, which are explicitly mentioned in the Bill of Rights, had become more of a default option than something people would seek out.

"Restaurants started offering French fries with food because they're super cheap, not because they're fabulous," Tom says. "We said 'Let's do it. Let's take them off.'"

The big subtraction turned out to be more of a tempest in a fry pot. While customers continued to order French fries, the serving staff learned to redirect them to the smashed potatoes instead. Over a year after the Battle of the Fry, sales are busier than ever.

"We just built a diversion tactic," Tom says. "We never really had any complaints." **DG**

MEET OUR SUPPLIERS

Our suppliers really mean a lot to us. 33% of all of our food comes directly from small, local suppliers, and that number gets higher when you consider the fact that our large distributors often source locally as well. Here's a list of what we are working on. Expect it to grow over time.

- Rainforest Alliance Organic Coffee – roasted and supplied locally from **Alakef Coffee**
- Herbal tea blends from **Anahata Herbal Apothecary**
- Fair trade – organic teas
- Cage-free organic eggs
- Organic salad greens
- Organic whole wheat & white flour
- Milk and cream in returnable bottles and butter from **Dahl's Sunrise Dairy** in Babbitt, MN
- All natural sour cream
- Hot cocoa made with real milk and organic Dutch cocoa
- Whitefish from **Lake Superior Fish Company**
- Smoked salmon by Eric Goerdt at **Northern Waters Smokehaus**
- Local produce from **Bayfield Apple Co., Brickyard Creek Farm, Hammarlund Nursery, Meadowbrook Cranberry Co**.
- Organic produce from **Northern Harvest Farm, Sawtooth, Mora Produce, Food Farm, Max Organics, Seeds of Success, Comfort Community Foods**
- Organic produce, pickles, and jelly from Kathy Jensen – **Talmadge Farms**
- All grass fed beef burgers from Mark Thell – **4 Quarters Holdings**
- Bison from **Quarter Master Buffalo** in Esko
- Wild rice from Northern Minnesota
- **Lifeway** Kefir for kids
- Organic produce from the **UMD Farm**
- **Gerber Amish Chicken** -Cage free, no chlorine wash
- Wild Alaskan salmon supplied by the **Rogotzke Family**
- Pure maple syrup harvested locally and supplied by the **Rogotzke Family**
- Honey from Ike Strohmayer – **Mirror Lake Beeworks**
- Honey from Marge and Don Korhonen – **Korhonen Apiaries**
- Organic bread and buns from **Positively 3rd Street Bakery**
- Local baked goods from **Johnson's Bakery**
- Tomatoes from **Bay Produce** in Superior, WI
- Eggs from **Promised Land Farm** in Carlton, MN
- Blueberries from the Dale family – **Highland Valley Farm**, Bayfield, WI
- Duck from Christian Gasset – **Au Bon Canard** - Caledonia, MN
- Nitrate free all natural turkey breast
- Homemade caramel sauce, hot fudge, jams, peanut butter, ketchup, mustard and BBQ sauce
- Homemade vinaigrettes made simply with olive oil
- All natural lemonade made from lemons, water and sugar
- Our artwork has been purchased from local artists
- Our coffee mugs are locally made by Karin Kraemer at **Duluth Pottery**
- Between our three garden areas (parking lot hugelbed, on-site gardens, and urban farm), we also raise our own rabbits along with herbs and produce

ACKNOWLEDGEMENTS

I can't believe we're already finishing the second cookbook. First, I have to thank the top managers of the Duluth Grill—Dan, Jeff, Louis, and Don, thank you for constantly pushing locally grown, homemade food and friendly service. It's not an exaggeration to say that the entire Duluth food scene is a better place because of your efforts. Tom and Jaima, thank you for having the vision to turn an Embers into a local foods legend in the first place. And finally, thank you to all the employees of Duluth Grill. Whether you're in the kitchen, dining room, or farm, you're a big part of what makes the restaurant so great.

I owe a lot to our four home cooks/recipe testers: Luisa Johnson, Sarah (and Dennis) Chambers, and Tiffany Kuchar. I obviously wasn't going to cook 100+ recipes myself, even recipes as tasty as these. I especially owe a debt of thanks to my brother Michael Lillegard, since not only was he my go-to guy for recipes that trickled in later in the process, I was also having him bake bread for the bakery we own together and be a subcontractor for a different project at the same time. Sorry you didn't get a summer vacation this year, but remember the end goal: Scrooge McDuck's vault or Smaug's hoard (minus the Arkenstone).

I have to thank my meticulous assistant, Olya Pavlova, who put the recipes in order and checked for errors. As much as it pains me to do this, I do take final responsibility for any mistakes.

Alicia, you've been a great wife. You have too many positives to list here, but a couple of highlights are how you schlepped to faraway cities with me on our book signing tour even though you were pregnant, and also how you told me "if I'm going to be a housewife, I'm going to up my cooking game" and started cooking more Duluth Grill recipes at home. I would thank our baby daughter Ruby, but honestly, she didn't exactly help with this project.

Rick and Rolf, you're not only amazing at photography and design, but you've got the years of experience and now the patience to deal with an occasionally overenthusiastic young author. This is a very good thing.

The final thanks goes to the customers of the Duluth Grill and anyone who's purchased, read, or reviewed this or the first cookbook. You vote with your wallets every time you buy a book or eat at a restaurant. Thanks for making what I'll call the exact right choice. Now go ahead and have some homemade ice cream. You deserve it!

—***Robert Lillegard***

INDEX